ALSO BY DAVID TALBOT
*Brothers: The Hidden History
of the Kennedy Years*

ALSO BY SPAIN RODRIGUEZ
Che: A Graphic Biography

Devil Dog

The Amazing True Story of the Man Who Saved America

BY DAVID TALBOT

WITH ORIGINAL ILLUSTRATIONS BY SPAIN RODRIGUEZ

DESIGNED BY NORMA TENNIS
PRODUCED BY KAREN CROFT

SIMON & SCHUSTER
New York   London   Toronto   Sydney

Simon & Schuster
1230 Avenue of the Americas
New York, NY 10020

First Simon & Schuster hardcover edition October 2010

SIMON & SCHUSTER and colophon are registered trademarks
of Simon & Schuster, Inc.

For information about special discounts for bulk purchases,
please contact Simon & Schuster Special Sales at
1-866-506-1949 or business@simonandschuster.com

The Simon & Schuster Speakers Bureau can bring authors
to your live event. For more information or to book
an event contact the Simon & Schuster Speakers Bureau at
1-866-248-3049 or visit our website at www.simonspeakers.com

Designed by Norma Tennis

Manufactured in China

1   3   5   7   9   10   8   6   4   2

Library of Congress Cataloging-in-Publication Data

Talbot, David.
Devil dog: the amazing true story of the man who saved America /
by David Talbot; with original illustrations by Spain Rodriguez.
—1st Simon & Schuster hardcover ed.
p.   cm.
1. Butler, Smedley D. (Smedley Darlington), 1881–1940.
2. Generals—United States—Biography. 3. United States Marine Corps—
Officers—Biography. 4. United States—History, Military—20th century.
5. Philadelphia (Pa.)—History—20th century.
6. United States—History—1933–1945. 7. United States—Politics and government—1933–1945. 8. Philadelphia (Pa.)—Biography. I. Title.
VE25.B88T35 2010
359.9'6092—dc22
[B]
2010005897

ISBN 978-1-4391-0902-1

Art and photo credits can be found on page 149.

Acknowledgments

The idea for the Pulp History series came to my sister, the talented and effervescent Margaret Talbot, and me during the cocktail hour in a midtown Manhattan restaurant—that magic hour when so many schemes and dreams take wing. This was the lightbulb that suddenly clicked over our heads: we would find a way to bring untold history stories to life, working with comics artists, illustrators and designers to fully exploit the lush possibilities of the printed page. As writers, we wanted the words to play a more important role than they do in graphic novels. But by adding a visual dimension to our true stories—and portraying history in all its terrible and beautiful glory—we thought we could make the past shine through the shadows for a new generation of readers.

The next day, our brainstorm still seemed to make sense. So we promptly took the idea to Simon & Schuster, where an entirely sober David Rosenthal and Priscilla Painton gave it an enthusiastic welcome. Priscilla has long been an ardent supporter of all things Talbot, and we both return her ardor in full.

Margaret and I owe David, Priscilla and their Simon & Schuster team—especially *Devil Dog* "point man" Michael Szczerban—our deepest thanks for helping make our bubbly dream come true.

We must also single out our Talbot Players colleague, the indispensable Karen Croft, who acted as "executive producer" on *Devil Dog,* marshaling the resources of our fledgling media company, keeping her gimlet eye on budgets and deadlines and, most important, helping maintain the highest creative standards.

We must also sing the praises of our designer, Norma Tennis, who gave the book its unique look and feel and whose vision and artistry are stamped on every page. Norma has the gifts of a fine artist, and—fortunately for us—the temperament of a saint, meeting every design challenge we hurled her way with cheerful equanimity.

We are indebted to Edith Wehle, the granddaughter of Smedley Darlington Butler, for opening the Butler family home to us and granting us access to memorabilia and personal correspondence, including Butler's courtship letters to his future wife, Ethel Conway Peters. Edith is a vigilant keeper of the Butler flame, and our path toward understanding Butler was greatly smoothed by her generosity.

My wife, Camille Peri, stands at the wild heart of everything I do. She is the first person subjected to my Mr. Toad–like manias, and is always a source of wise and loving counsel. She was the first to read *Devil Dog* in its entirety and, as always, brought her finely tuned skills as a writer and editor to the task.

Research assistance was provided by the staffs of the Alfred M. Gray Research Center at the Quantico Marine Base Library, the Free Library of Philadelphia and the National Archives and Records Administration, as well as by Cliff Callahan and Susan Strange.

Finally, I must give a big bear hug to my *Devil Dog* collaborator, the legendary Manuel "Spain" Rodriguez, one of the great masters of modern comix. Spain—who brings an infectious, boyish glee to everything he does—made this one of the most fun professional escapades of my life. Spain's deep and always surprising knowledge of history, in all its infinite weirdness, and his love of great unsung heroes like Smedley Butler made him the perfect companion on this journey into the past.

To those who fight in America's wars,
and to those who question why
we constantly fight them

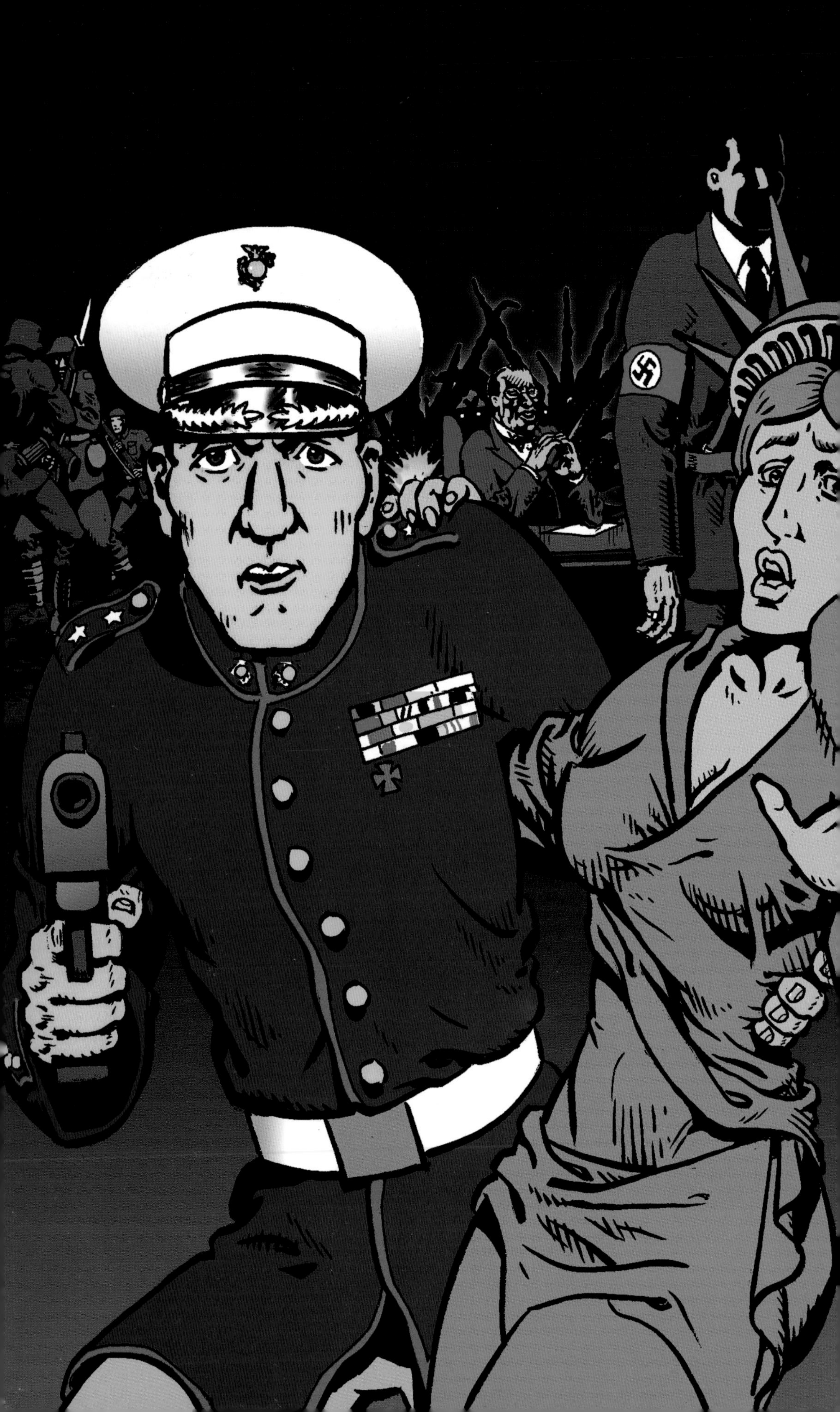

Contents

Devil Dog

Boys dream of war.

In their mind's eye, they fight as bravely as Sir Galahad or the Three Musketeers. But they're not supposed to really go to war. Smedley Darlington Butler did, when he was just 16. He ran off to join the marines and fight the dastardly Spaniards in Cuba. He never knew a Spaniard; he'd never been far from home. It was all just picture books and recruiting posters and rippling flags to him.

In the end, he would turn his own life into a storybook. But not the kind he grew up reading.

Smedley Butler would fight valiantly all over the world—Cuba, the Philippines, China, Nicaragua, Haiti, France. He would lead men into battle against impossible odds; he would be decorated more than any other marine in his day. But it was not until many years later that Smedley Butler finally got to fight for his country.

He was the man who saved America. And he did it right at home.

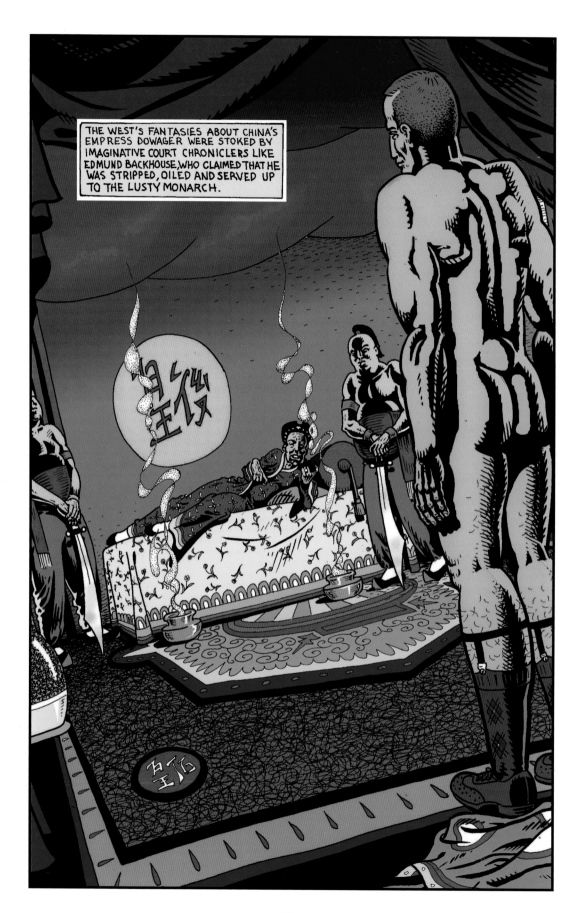

THE WEST'S FANTASIES ABOUT CHINA'S EMPRESS DOWAGER WERE STOKED BY IMAGINATIVE COURT CHRONICLERS LIKE EDMUND BACKHOUSE, WHO CLAIMED THAT HE WAS STRIPPED, OILED AND SERVED UP TO THE LUSTY MONARCH.

Act 1

THE YEAR OF
THE DRAGON

HEBEI PROVINCE, CHINA, AUGUST 1900

The sun was a furnace as young Smedley Darlington Butler and his fellow soldiers trudged across the scorched and dusty plains of northern China. There were no trees to shade them from the merciless glare. There were no cool, clean waters to relieve their terrible thirst, just the sluggish, yellow muck of the Pei Ho River, whose meandering path they wearily followed. The wagon road on which they were marching took a perversely crooked route, as all Chinese roads did, because evil spirits were said to fly on straight lines. At times the frustrated soldiers tried to shorten their march by cutting through the cornfields that lined the road. But closed in by the dense stalks where no breeze could find them, the men felt even more suffocated by the heat.

As the hours went by and the sun reached its full fury, the soldiers abandoned more and more of what they had brought. Blankets, tents, shovels, ponchos all began to litter the roadside. And then they began to strip off their very uniforms, until some were nearly naked except for the rifles and ammunition belts strung across their bodies.

And still, they pushed on toward Peking, driven by the terror that they would be too late, that their countrymen—men, women and children—would be overrun and slaughtered by the Chinese hordes that had been laying siege to the capital city's foreign compounds. The stories had been racing around the world for months, horrifying newspaper readers across America and Europe: stories of Christian missionaries and their families being tortured by "Oriental demons" in the most unspeakable ways—death

17

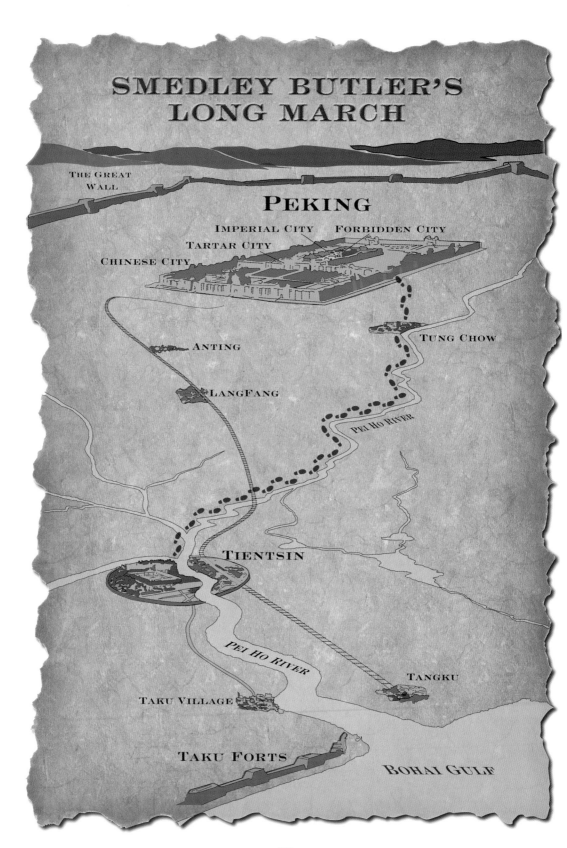

SMEDLEY BUTLER'S
LONG MARCH

THE GREAT
WALL

PEKING

IMPERIAL CITY   FORBIDDEN CITY
TARTAR CITY
CHINESE CITY

ANTING

LANGFANG

TUNG CHOW

PEI HO RIVER

TIENTSIN

PEI HO RIVER

TANGKU

TAKU VILLAGE

TAKU FORTS

BOHAI GULF

Devil Dog

by a thousand cuts and other exquisite agonies, described in titillating detail. Some newspapers even declared that all foreigners in Peking had already been horribly massacred. "The Streets Ran Blood," blared the *Topeka State Journal*.

China had gone mad. The Empress Dowager, the cunning monarch who ruled the Manchu court, was reported to have unleashed a mysterious martial arts cult known as the Boxers on the "foreign devils" residing in the Middle Kingdom. Despite their humble, peasant origins, the Boxers were thought by their countrymen—including the Empress herself—to possess otherworldly powers that could withstand even the bullets and guns of the Western powers. With their long pigtails, red sashes and curved swords, the Boxers struck fear in the round-eyed missionaries and merchants who seemed to be overrunning China. But they were an inspiration to the Chinese people who felt humiliated by the Western intruders.

Now the armies of the Western world were marching on Peking, some 16,000 soldiers from eight nations. They had left the port city of Tientsin on August 4, some 97 miles away. If they were in time, this remarkable military procession would be a rescue mission. If not, they would be a blazing sword of vengeance.

A mong the marching soldiers was 18-year-old U.S. Marine Corps Lieutenant Smedley Butler, who commanded a company of 45 enlisted men. Butler had already been wounded once in China, shot in the right leg during the vicious battle for Tientsin. He did not know what to expect as he and his men prepared to set off on their desperate march for Peking. He did not know if his luck would stand and whether he would ever again see his mother and father and his younger brothers, Samuel and Horace (whom he called "Horrid"). On the morning before they marched, Butler wrote his mother, Maud, a letter, using the plain language of the Quaker faith in which he was raised.

My darling Mother,
We start in one hour for Peking. Preparations all made, expect to run against 30,000 chinamen to-morrow morning. Don't be worried about me. If I am killed, I gave my life for women and children just as dear to some poor devil as thee and Horrid are to me.
Lots of love to all. Good bye.
Thy son,
Smedley D. Butler.

Butler looked too young to die. He was a bantam rooster of a boy-man, measuring

DAMSELS IN DISTRESS: THE ARMIES OF THE WESTERN WORLD DESCENDED ON PEKING AFTER HEARING OF OUTRAGES AGAINST "CHRISTIAN WOMEN."

a scrappy 5-foot-9 and weighing no more than 140 pounds. His bird beak was the first thing you noticed about him, and then his penetrating eyes, which went along with his pugnacious attitude. You wouldn't know it to look at the sinewy young man, with the massive marine tattoo carved into his chest, but he was a Philadelphia blueblood, the scion of three prominent Pennsylvania families who traced their ancestry back to William Penn's colony. Both of his grandfathers were politically connected bankers, and his father, Thomas Butler, was a powerful congressman, who—despite the family's devout Quaker roots—used his platform on the Naval Affairs Committee to prod turn-of-the-century America into becoming a military power.

Still, Congressman Butler was appalled when his teenage son announced that he was leaving the bosom of his distinguished family to join the toughest fighting arm of the military, the United States Marine Corps. But there was nothing he or the boy's mother could do to stop him. At the time, Smedley was enrolled at prestigious Haverford School, the training ground for the sons of wealthy Quaker families. In the classroom, he was as bored and restless as young Tom Sawyer.

Maybe Smedley, with his utter disinterest in school, knew he would never equal his father in the marble halls of Washington or the plush salons of Main Line Philadelphia.

ALL IS LOST SAVE HONOR.

SPAIN'S SUNSET.

HYSTERIA SWEPT THE **AMERICAN PRESS** DURING THE WARS AGAINST **SPAIN** AND **CHINA.**

So he would find another way to become a man and impress his father. He would become a man of "action, not books," in his words.

When the USS *Maine* blew up in Havana Harbor in February 1898 and war fever swept through the country, that settled it. Smedley joined the crowds that built bonfires and sang out, "Remember the *Maine,* to Hell with Spain!" Suddenly school seemed even more "stupid and unnecessary," he thought.

At 16, Smedley announced to his mother that she must accompany him to the marine headquarters in Washington, D.C., and give permission for him to join up, or he would lie about his age and enlist anyway.

And so, after six weeks of training, Second Lieutenant Smedley Butler finally got the flashy uniform that had dazzled him when he first saw a marine officer strolling by on the streets of Philadelphia—the one with the dark-blue coat, and sky-blue trousers emblazoned with scarlet stripes down the seams. And, in July, he was shipped off to fight in Cuba—the splendid little war against the dying Spanish empire that would turn America into a young empire.

The fresh-faced marine officer arrived too late to see much action. It would not be until two years later, in a land even farther away—China, the ancient Middle Kingdom—that Smedley Butler would fully experience the savage education that is war.

When the allied forces marched out of Tientsin for Peking, to the triumphal strains of a U.S. Army band, Butler marveled at the variety of flapping banners and crisp uniforms on display—the French Zouaves in red and blue, the Royal Welsh Fusiliers with their five black ribbons hanging from their collars, the turbaned Sikhs, the Cossack cavalrymen in their white tunics and shiny black topboots. The colorful military pageant represented the combined, fearsome might of the imperial powers: Great Britain, Germany, Austria, France, Italy, Russia, Japan and the United States. Never before had the world seen such a union of lethal force.

But as the days went by, and the sun beat down mercilessly, the procession grew ragged and dispirited. The troops choked on clouds of dust kicked up by the rumbling artillery carriages and were besieged by dark swarms of flies and bloodthirsty mosquitoes. The American soldiers were especially parched because they had brought fewer water tanks than their allies and the water sterilizing machines that Washington had promised had still not arrived.

Butler warned his men not to drink from the muddy wells they found in the villages along the way, fearing they had been poisoned by the Boxers. And the Pei Ho River looked equally putrid. But mad with thirst, Butler's marines could not help themselves and they sometimes gulped frantically from the river, straining the sallow water with their handkerchiefs and holding their noses to block the river's stench. To their horror, they would sometimes see headless bodies floating by—the handiwork of the Japanese soldiers leading the allied column, who not only cleared away Boxer resistance but also decapitated helpless Chinese villagers.

For the most part, the American soldiers refrained from the cruelty that seemed to come easily to their allies, especially the Japanese, Germans and Russians. Many of these soldiers felt they had the divine right of vengeance. "Spare nobody," Kaiser Wilhelm II had commanded the German expeditionary force as they sailed from Bremerhaven. "Use your weapons so that for a thousand years hence no Chinaman

ALL FOREIGNERS IN PEKING DEAD

All Missionaries and Converts Being Exterminated

PRIESTS HORRIBLY TORTURED

Wrapped in Kerosene-Soaked Cotton and Roasted to Death

Every Foreigner in Pe-Chi-Li Believed to be Dead—Twelve Missionaries Slain Near Ning-Po.

SHANGHAI, July 30—The Shanghai correspondent of The Daily Express, under yesterday's date, wires as follows:

"Sheng now admits that he has had telegrams since July 19 announcing that every foreigner in Pao-ting-Foo was murdered, including forty British, French, and American missionaries, and announcing also that two French Jesuits and a thousand converts have been massacred at Kwangping-Foo, on the borders of Shan-Tung and Pe-chi-Li.

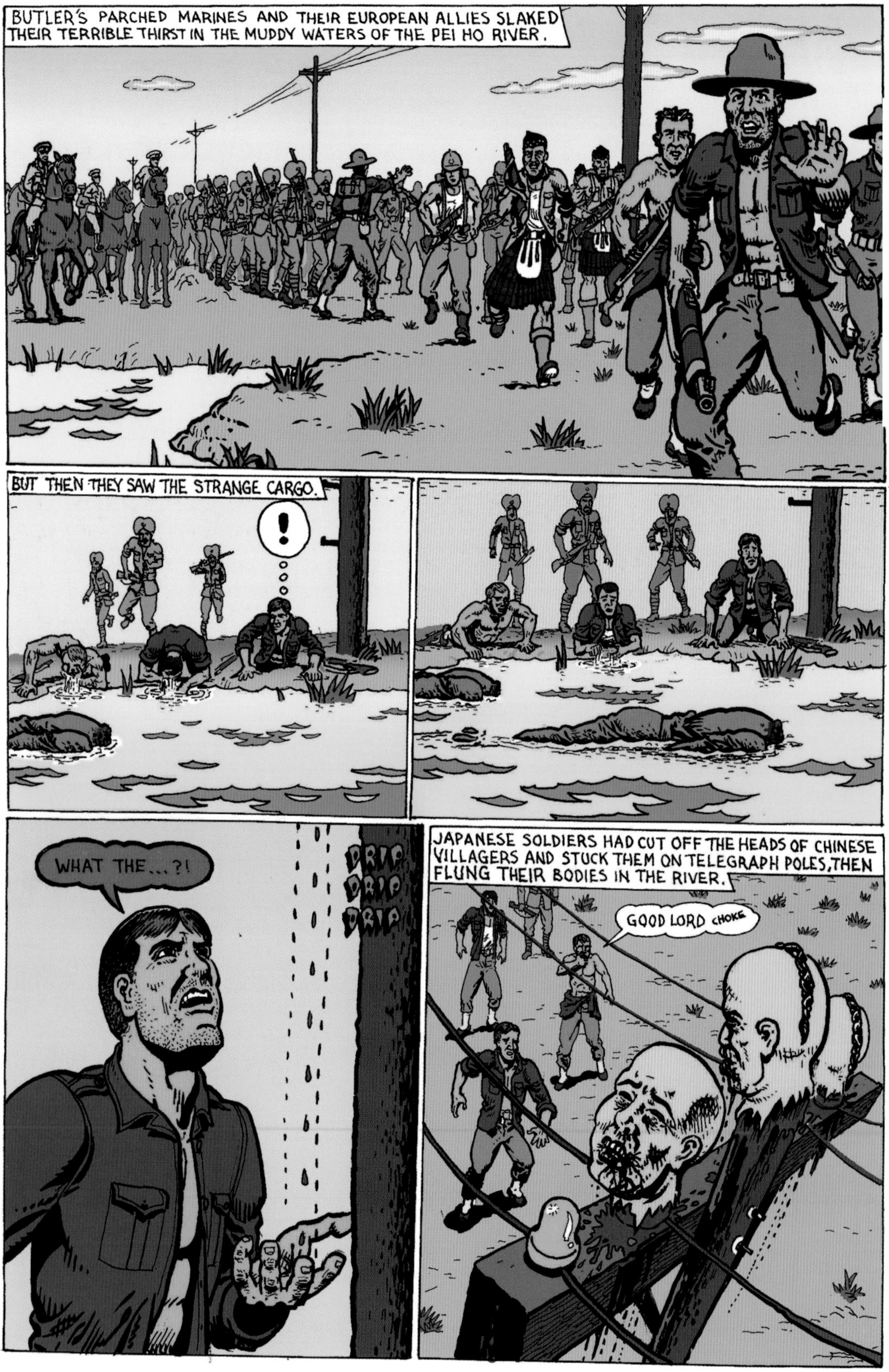
BUTLER'S PARCHED MARINES AND THEIR EUROPEAN ALLIES SLAKED THEIR TERRIBLE THIRST IN THE MUDDY WATERS OF THE PEI HO RIVER.
BUT THEN THEY SAW THE STRANGE CARGO.
!
WHAT THE...?!
DRIP DRIP DRIP
JAPANESE SOLDIERS HAD CUT OFF THE HEADS OF CHINESE VILLAGERS AND STUCK THEM ON TELEGRAPH POLES, THEN FLUNG THEIR BODIES IN THE RIVER.
GOOD LORD CHOKE

will dare look askance at any German. Open the way for civilization once and for all."

Chinese girls threw themselves down wells rather than fall into the hands of the foreign demons. The Chinese imperial soldiers and Boxers fighting desperately to block the allied advance were also terrified of being captured by the foreign invaders. When they were wounded, they would crawl into the cornfields to die, instead of being captured alive. But some were not so lucky.

Henry Savage Landor, the celebrated British writer and explorer, witnessed one particularly brutal incident on the way to Peking. Landor knew something about torture: while traveling in forbidden Tibet in 1897, he had been captured and subjected to torches and the stretching rack. But he was particularly disturbed by what he saw one day in China, when a prisoner fell into the hands of American soldiers.

"Take him away and do with him what you damned please," an American officer told the soldiers.

The doomed man was then dragged under a railway bridge, where he was punched and kicked by the Americans, only to be replaced by a French soldier, who shot him in the face. Still breathing and moaning, the prisoner was then stomped on by a Japanese soldier. Clinging miraculously to life, he was then stripped naked by the mob of soldiers to see if he possessed any of the supernatural charms that Boxers claimed to have. "For nearly an hour, the fellow lay in this dreadful condition," Landor recalled, "with hundreds of soldiers leaning over him to get a glimpse of his agony, and going into roars of laughter as he made ghastly contortions in his delirium."

As Landor noted, this barbarous behavior deeply pained most of the American boys, "who were as a rule extremely humane, even at times extravagantly gracious, towards the enemy."

Here's how these boys left home, saying goodbye to their dearest ones, uncertain if they would ever set eyes on one another again. Here's how they always leave home. The mothers and sisters and sweethearts gathered, ashen-faced, around them, in their barracks on the Presidio overlooking the San Francisco Bay or on Governors Island in New York Harbor, just hours before their soldier boys set sail for China. These women wanted one last embrace, heart against heart, that they could feel longer than death. But some were too frantic to keep still.

"Oh! Why did you go and enlist, Charlie? And now you have to go and leave me and the child alone," wept one young woman. Her Charlie was with the Fifteenth U.S. Infantry, stationed at Governors Island, and a reporter overheard their agonized farewell.

"It had to be done, Lizzie," Charlie told his young wife as she clung to his chest. "You know I could not find any work."

And weeks later, these boys found themselves tramping through an inferno somewhere halfway around the world, in a cornfield filled with reeking corpses. They were confused about how they had ended up there, why they were killing these odd people whose language sounded like birds. And when they fell in battle, cut down by a Chinese soldier defending his homeland, Chaplain Groves would write down their name and regiment and bury the information in a sealed bottle next to the soldier. It was the only way these American boys could later be identified and sent back home to rest in eternity.

In such a wretched place, with death hovering everywhere, soldiers have only one another. They pray that their officers are decent and wise and will not get them killed. The men of First Battalion, Company A, USMC, were lucky to have Lieutenant Butler marching at the head of their column.

Despite his privileged background and tender age, Butler acted like one of them—the roughneck immigrants, hard-luck cases and refugees from the law who made up the Marine Corps rank and file. He drank as hard as they did, and he swore as blue as they did. And, most important, he was the kind of man who would put his own life on the line for you. That's why he was dragging a gimp leg on the long road to Peking—he had taken the bullet in his right thigh while carrying a wounded private to safety during the fight for Tientsin.

As Butler shuffled through the choking heat and dust, his injured thigh throbbed with each step. But he still did not hesitate to share his food and water with his men, or to help carry their loads when they seemed about to drop in their tracks from heat exhaustion. One of the crusty Civil War veterans who had schooled Butler in the ways of the military during his Cuba expedition had told him that if an officer helps carry a weary soldier's load, he wins the man's loyalty for life. And Butler's men—even the ones old enough to be his father—soon grew devoted to their teenage leader.

Some of the European officers and the Western correspondents accompanying their advance, who had grown used to the comforts of imperial duty, brought along

THE IMPERIAL SOLDIERS WERE TOLD THAT THEY HAD THE DIVINE RIGHT OF VENGEANCE.

their Chinese "boys" to cook for them. These servants would go foraging in the countryside, bringing back poultry and pork and vegetables for savory meals, which their Western masters washed down with wine and bottled water. But Butler and his marines were forced to subsist on salted bacon and hardtack. American soldiers were fed decently while in barracks—but in the field, they ate miserably.

One evening, after his company had set up camp, a desperate Butler decided to relieve the monotony of their diet and backtrack four miles to the rear, to a watermelon patch they had passed earlier in the day. Butler and a group of soldiers quickly fell upon the melons, splitting them open with their swords and greedily devouring their sweet red flesh. Butler himself ate 13 of them. Then he and his band loaded themselves with as many melons as they could carry for the rest of the company and started back to camp. Suddenly, as they were passing a village, Butler's stomach was wrenched by cramps, from the surfeit of fruit or from the brackish water of the Pei Ho River that he had not been able to resist in his thirst.

Butler doubled over and started to sink to the ground. But then he caught himself,

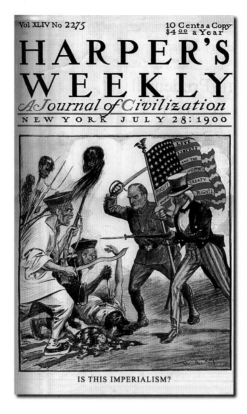

Vol XLIV No 2275   10 Cents a Copy $4.00 a Year

HARPER'S WEEKLY
A Journal of Civilization
NEW YORK   JULY 28:1900

IS THIS IMPERIALISM?

PRESIDENT MCKINLEY
DEFENDED
THE INVASION AS A
RESCUE MISSION.

as his eyes fell on a grisly specter. Two Japanese soldiers were nailed to a door, with their eyes and tongues cut out. The Chinese had wreaked revenge on their tormentors. Butler quickly got to his feet. "We beat it back to our column in double quick time."

After nine days, the allies reached Tungchow, 12 miles from Peking, where the Chinese imperial forces made their final stand to stop the Western drive on the capital. General Li Ping-heng, the old patriot in command of China's resistance, watched wretchedly as his ranks were depleted by deserters. "From youth to old age I have experienced many wars, but never saw things like these. The situation is getting out of control," General Li despaired in a final message to the Peking court. The following day, after his army was overrun, the old general swallowed poison. The allies' path to Peking was now clear.

The assault on Peking would fully test Smedley Butler. A young officer does not know what he is really made of until he endures this kind of crucible. What is the essence of brave leadership? One of Butler's comrades in the China relief expedition, an army colonel named A. S. Daggett,

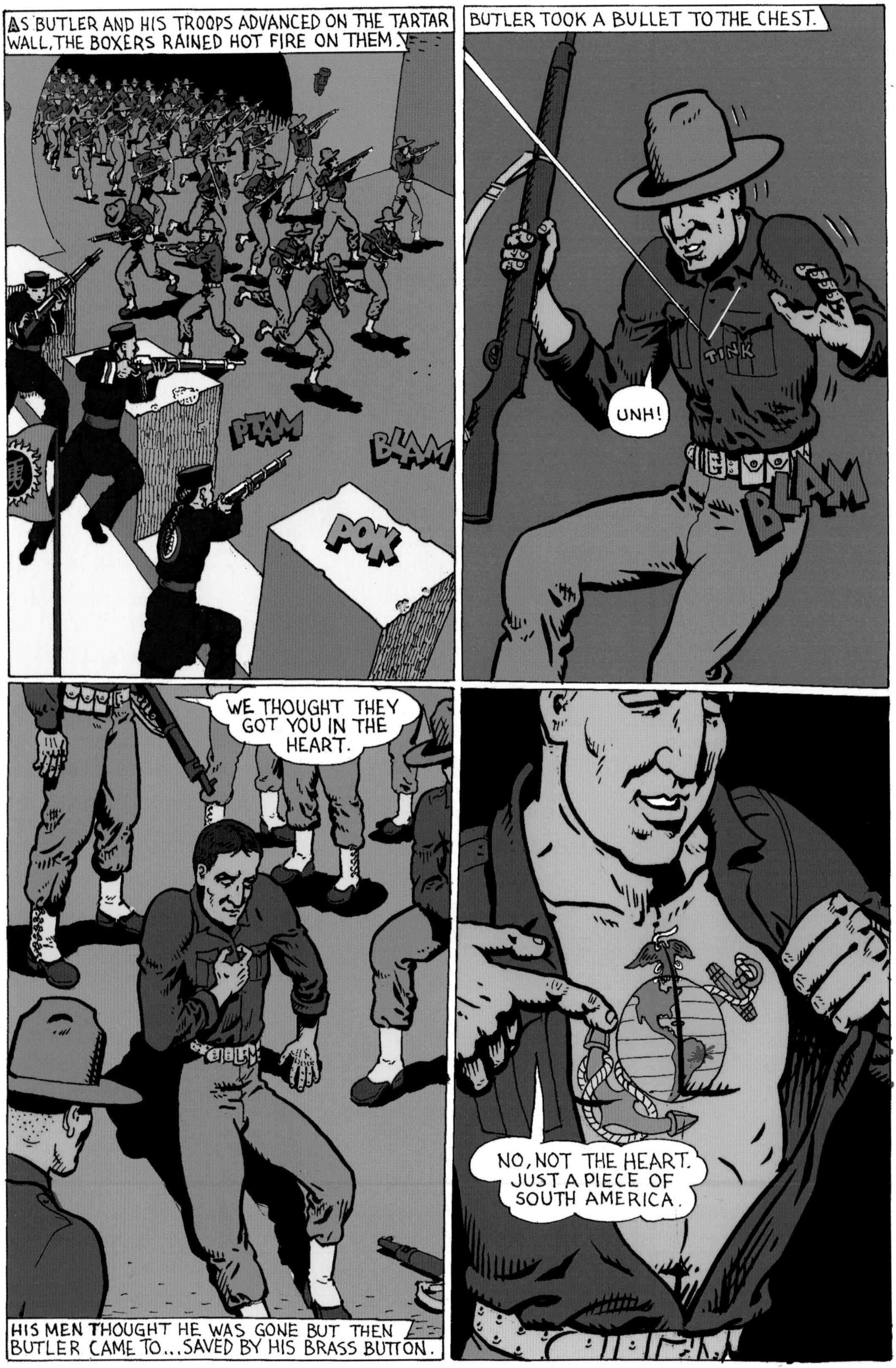
AS BUTLER AND HIS TROOPS ADVANCED ON THE TARTAR WALL, THE BOXERS RAINED HOT FIRE ON THEM.
PTAM
BLAM
POK
BUTLER TOOK A BULLET TO THE CHEST.
TINK
UNH!
BLAM
WE THOUGHT THEY GOT YOU IN THE HEART.
HIS MEN THOUGHT HE WAS GONE BUT THEN BUTLER CAME TO... SAVED BY HIS BRASS BUTTON.
NO, NOT THE HEART. JUST A PIECE OF SOUTH AMERICA.

later reflected on this in his memoir. He had seen officers grow excited in battle and seek to smother their fears with "bluster" and "boisterous actions." These men, remarked Daggett, "will never inspire men around them with confidence."

"But there are men," he went on, "who have complete mastery of themselves; they remain calm and cool under the most exciting circumstances, and inspire all about them with the same spirit. They know that success against a formidable enemy is generally gained by intelligent direction. They, therefore, endeavor to restrain the impulsive nature in their commands up to the last possible moment; but when the moment arrives for the assault, they let loose their impulsive natures and rush like a thunderbolt against the enemy and carry everything before them. They use intelligence and impulse; but, knowing that the effectiveness of the latter is of short duration, they husband it so that it shall not be exhausted before it has accomplished its contemplated work. Such men are born commanders."

This was the type of leader that Smedley Butler turned out to be.

The allied forces had decided to rest for a day some three miles outside Peking, to allow their soldiers—whose ranks were decimated by sunstroke, dysentery and typhoid—to regain their strength. But as they neared the ancient walled city—with its jade and gold treasures—greed spread like fever through the West's imperial armies and the Russians stole a march, setting out in the dead of night to take the city by surprise. When the other Western powers discovered this duplicity, they too charged in a frenzy towards the city.

Butler and his troops came upon Peking at dawn, after slogging by night through a torrential rainstorm. Drenched and shivering, they stared at the massive battlements looming before them in the mist. "Peking was all walls, and every wall held possible danger for us," Butler would later write.

First came the great stone wall of the outer Chinese City, then the 40-foot wall of the Tartar City, then the red wall of the Imperial City, and finally the ultimate prize—the fabled Forbidden City, where the yellow-tiled palaces of the Empress Dowager and her court gleamed mysteriously.

As Butler and his troops reached the walls of the Chinese City, pausing by a gate where ducks swam serenely in a nearby pond, they saw that the Russians' stealth attack had not paid off. Chinese soldiers were pinning down the Russians by firing from atop the Tartar Wall. Butler's commanding officer, Major Littleton Waller, ordered him to gather his company and charge through the gate. "Drive those pests off the wall," Waller growled, sweeping his arm toward the Chinese sharpshooters.

Butler and his men stormed through the gate, rushing past their Russian allies. The Chinese blazed down at them. Suddenly Butler spun around in a circle, struck in the chest by a bullet. When he came to, he was on the ground, struggling for breath. "He's shot through the heart," one of the marines gathered around him said. "No, not the heart," gasped the young lieutenant.

Butler had been saved by the second button on his marine blouse, which deflected the bullet. For years after, he would carry the flattened brass button in his pocket as a lucky charm. Butler's chest, which was turning ink-black from the blow, ached and he was coughing up blood. But he insisted on rejoining his men as they continued their successful charge.

That evening, despite his injuries, Butler was intent upon slipping into the Legation Quarter, which had been liberated earlier in the day by the army's Fourteenth Infantry. He wanted to meet the American diplomats

TEDDY AND TWAIN
THE FIGHT FOR AMERICA'S SOUL

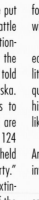

The loudest roar for American Empire in 1900 came from the toothy, brash rising politician Teddy Roosevelt. Two years before, as the young assistant navy secretary, TR had pushed the country into the Spanish-American War—even rounding up a colorful mix of polo-playing dandies and Texas cowboys nicknamed "the Rough Riders" to lead into battle. During the 1900 presidential race, as Republican president William McKinley's vice presidential running mate, Roosevelt led the charge for an "expansionist" America, robustly defending the occupation of the Philippines and the Boxer campaign.

"Expansion means in the end not war, but peace," he told a boisterous campaign crowd in St. Paul, Minnesota. Granting freedom to Philippine rebels or backing down from the Boxers in China, shouted Roosevelt, "would be precisely like giving independence to the wildest tribe of Apaches in Arizona."

The 1900 presidential race became a referendum on American imperialism, which the Democratic National Platform declared was "the paramount issue of the campaign." Imperialism, the Democrats stated, "meant conquest abroad and intimidation and oppression at home."

The Democratic candidate, crusading populist William Jennings Bryan, was a silver-tongued orator and he put up an impassioned fight. The battle over American interventionism was a crusade for the country's very soul, he told a rally in Lincoln, Nebraska. "When you go to the polls to vote, remember that you are an American citizen. For 124 years this nation has held before the world the light of liberty." Don't let this light be extinguished in the jungles of the Philippines, Bryan implored his fellow citizens.

"I am a Boxer."
-Mark Twain

In the end, the American people chose the dazzling vision of global power painted by Roosevelt. The Republican ticket won an overwhelming victory in November. But the voices of dissent were not silenced.

The most persuasive voice raised against the country's expansionist policies was that of Mark Twain. He had a simple way of skewering the logic of imperialism that made it seem distinctly un-American. Shortly after the triumph

Rootin' tootin' Teddy Roosevelt

of the McKinley-Roosevelt ticket, Twain appeared before an overflow gathering of educators in New York City and announced, "I am a Boxer."

"Why should not China be free from the foreigners, who are only making trouble on her soil?" remarked America's most beloved writer and humorist. "If they would only all go home, what a pleasant place China would be for the Chinese! China never wanted foreigners any more than foreigners wanted Chinamen, and on this question I am with the Boxers every time. The Boxer is a patriot."

Twain and Roosevelt inevitably squared off against each other. "Mr. Roosevelt is the Tom Sawyer of the political world…always hunting for a chance to show off," quipped Twain after TR became president. Roosevelt, for his part, said that he would be glad to see peace lovers like Twain skinned alive.

Eventually, the power of celebrity outshined the two American icons' political differences. In 1905 Roosevelt invited his old foe to dine at the White House.

But to the end of his life, Twain remained an ardent enemy of the "pirate raids" undertaken by the United States and European powers against far-flung colonial realms. Imperial adventures always soil a conquering nation, Twain wryly observed, leaving her "soul full of meanness, her pocket full of boodle, and her mouth full of pious hypocrisies."

and missionaries for whom he and his men had risked their lives. Butler and some fellow officers crawled through the Water Gate, a foul-smelling open sewer, emerging in the sedate, grassy compound of the American mission.

It was an awkward encounter. The soldiers were a grimy, bedraggled lot after marching and fighting for ten days. But the diplomatic families who greeted them seemed to be stepping out of a garden party, well-groomed and decked out in the finest fashions. Some of the men wore starched shirts with high, glazed collars, fancy flannel suits and gaily colored ties. The besieged were clearly delighted to be rescued, and they had obviously endured hardships. But, as they mingled with the sweat-stained soldiers, some of the diplomatic corps had a sniffy attitude that their rescuers found insufferable.

"We dirty creatures thought these particular fellows silly and objectionable; they put on such patronizing airs that it made one almost feel sorry we had relieved them," said one rescuer. "They kept us at arm's length because we were not as smartly dressed as they, and kept looking at our attire in a way which suggested that we ought to be ashamed of ourselves for

not coming to relieve them without putting on our best clothes!"

Did Butler and his men fight and bleed for these coddled creatures of empire? Was this why they had tramped halfway around the globe?

The real reason for their mission emerged the next day, when the American soldiers were sent with bayonets drawn into the secret heart of Peking, where China's power and wealth were concentrated. By seizing China's imperial center, the United States and its allies would tighten their grip on the Middle Kingdom's vast resources.

CAPTURED BOXERS: THE WEST CALLED THEM "SAVAGES" BUT TO THE CHINESE THEY WERE PATRIOTS.

Early in the morning, General Adna Chaffee—the old mustachioed Indian fighter who commanded America's relief expedition—galloped up to the marine encampment under the Tartar Wall and ordered the men in blue to join with the Fourteenth Infantry to take the Imperial City. Throughout the day, Butler and the American forces engaged in vicious street fighting, huddling under Peking's vast walls while American artillery pieces blew down the thick wooden gates and iron bars that blocked their way, then charging through the gaping holes. It was gate to gate, courtyard to courtyard. And everywhere the soldiers rushed, they encountered

THE MAN-EATER OF PEKING

As a teenage concubine, it was said that she turned the Emperor of China into a drooling imbecile after a 72-hour sexual marathon. She poisoned her own son, the boy emperor Tung Chih, and other family rivals for the throne. She filled her court with sleek young men posing as eunuchs and then had them killed after they satisfied her rampant lust. These were some of the lurid stories that circulated in Peking's foreign legations about the Empress Dowager, Tzu Hsi, China's aging monarch during the Boxer Rebellion.

Many of these stories were the work of a brilliant Oxford-educated fantasist named Sir Edmund Backhouse—an embittered homosexual outcast from a prominent British family who found his way to China shortly before the uprising. Backhouse's wicked slander about the Empress worked its way into the Western press through George Morrison, the Peking correspondent for the *Times of London*, who employed the gifted linguist as a translator.

When anti-Western violence began sweeping China, European and American newspapers soon began blaming the Empress for the bloodshed. China, proclaimed the *New York Times*, is "hag-ridden by the malignant woman."

In truth, the Empress was a sad and isolated figure in her own court, manipulated by crafty princes and mandarins who pushed her into supporting the Boxers—a disastrous decision that the Western powers quickly exploited by invading China.

As the foreign armies reached the walls of Peking, the Empress prepared to flee, ransacking her closets for precious mementos, including a bloodstone that she thought shielded her from all dangers, clipping her long talons and dressing like a peasant woman to hide her identity. The flying bullets outside the Forbidden City sounded to her like "the crying of cats"—an animal she detested. As her caravan made its long journey into exile in the remote wastelands of northwestern China, the Empress wept the entire way and cursed those who had brought ruin upon the Middle Kingdom.

The Manchu dynasty never recovered from the Western invasion, and Tzu Hsi—who died in 1908—would be the last Empress of China.

But even in death, the Empress Dowager continued to be violated by Western sleaze-mongers, particularly Backhouse, whose pornographic imagination grew more flagrant with age. In the final months of his life, the bedridden "guru of Peking"—now sporting a long white beard and the silk robes of a mandarin—amused himself by writing a "memoir" of his affair with the Empress titled *Decadence Mandchoue*.

The book was filled with garish sexual escapades, including one evening of pleasure when the young Englishman was prepared for the 67-year-old Empress by her grand eunuch, who anointed his cock and balls with sandalwood—her favorite scent—and dressed him in a thigh-length cloak before leading him like a sacrificial lamb into her bedchamber. There she reclined, inspecting him under a blaze of candlelights, before issuing this imperial command: "My bed is cold... now exhibit to me your genitals for I know I shall love them." According to Backhouse, the Empress proved a formidable lover, who took great joy in wielding her exorbitant-sized clitoris like an erect penis against his backside.

In reality, it was the Empress who was ravaged by the West, which penetrated her kingdom—including her most secret and precious chambers—and took what it wanted.

blazing fire from the walled city's countless towers and dark corners.

While the Americans blasted their way through the Chinese defenses, they could not be certain of allied support behind them. After marching together for 10 days, the armies of the Western world were beginning to show their true imperial colors, jostling to be the first to plant their flags on top of the Empress Dowager's palace. As one U.S. Army battalion advanced on the Imperial City, a Russian company suddenly tried to cut them off, until the American major made it ominously clear that his men had the right of way. As another American unit blew apart a gate in the pink-walled Imperial City and prepared to plunge through, it suddenly came under fire from a French battery on the Tartar Wall—a bit of "friendly fire" that did not strike the Americans as accidental. Only after a furious General Chaffee dispatched an aide on horseback to shout violent oaths at the French artillery officer did the barrage on the advancing American soldiers finally halt.

The successful American charge on the Imperial City was propelled by the deadly effective artillery unit under the command of Captain H. J. Reilly. The artillery captain was beloved by his gunners, who worked at a frantic pace to blast through one walled fortress after the next. Reilly was also greatly admired by fellow officers like Butler. When the artillery captain fell in action, it was a particularly grievous blow for all those fighting alongside him. Butler was standing near Reilly as the captain shouted his final order. A bullet struck him in the mouth and knocked him backwards into the arms of Major Waller,

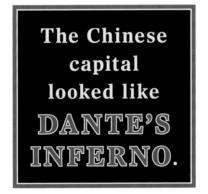

The Chinese capital looked like DANTE'S INFERNO.

his lifelong friend, where he died as Waller held him. Reilly's battle-hardened gunners began weeping, but continued to work their red-hot field pieces as tears streamed down their faces.

As they raced from courtyard to courtyard, the American soldiers beheld horrific scenes: packs of ravenous wolf-dogs fed on rotting corpses; entire families had committed suicide by hanging together from the rafters of their homes.

Butler and the American troops finally reached the walls of the Forbidden City—the innermost sanctuary of China's imperial dynasty. Through the holes in the walls, the soldiers could see glimpses of the paradise where the Empress and her court dwelled—lush lotus ponds spanned by marble bridges, dazzling golden pagodas. But then, just as the prize was within reach, old General Chaffee ordered his men to cease firing...and to withdraw!

The men couldn't believe their ears. By this point, the soldiers were no longer sure why they had been sent on this miserable mission on the other side of the earth. But they had come and they had done everything they were told to do. And when they were ordered to take the final bastion of Chinese power, they had responded with enormous grit and courage. As they shuffled away from the Forbidden City Wall, they swore bitterly, calling down the punishment of heaven and hell on the officers who treated them like chess pieces. But Lieutenant Butler was spared their fiery wrath. He was one of them, and he had been with them every step of the way.

The soldiers learned that the order to stop firing had come down from the diplomatic

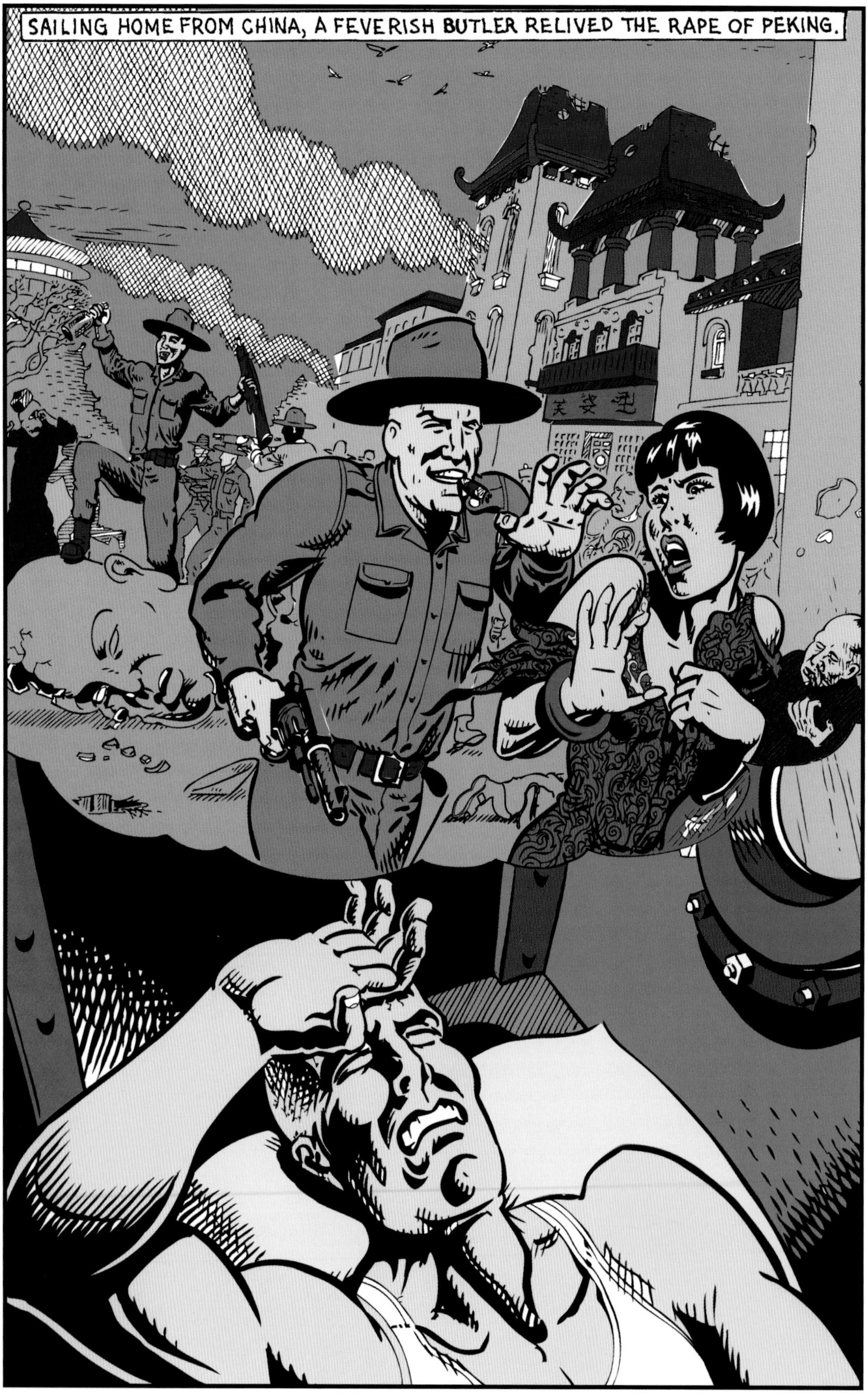
SAILING HOME FROM CHINA, A FEVERISH BUTLER RELIVED THE RAPE OF PEKING.

missions, because "it might offend the Chinese court." But by then, the Empress and her court had fled Peking for a remote sanctuary. The real reason that the American advance was halted, his officers told him, was that the other Western powers wanted to be assured of their share of the Forbidden City's spoils.

Days later, allied delegations assembled for a stately march into the Forbidden City, as a military band blared the national anthems of each victorious power. The Chinese attendants left behind by the Empress to watch over the royal grounds decided they had no choice but to be hospitable, and they greeted their conquerors with cups of tea as the uniformed columns marched through the gates. But the allies' military discipline soon broke down, and officers began snatching everything they could get their hands on in the imperial palaces, from jade ornaments to silk robes to gold goblets. One Western officer even swiped the necklace off one of the Chinese officials who was guiding him through the grounds. Others grabbed the teacups and plates out of the hands of the Chinese serving them. Even diplomats, missionaries and correspondents for prestigious newspapers joined in the looting.

Now the fever spread through the rank and file encamped throughout Peking. China was at their feet and the soldiers threw themselves on her. The German and Russian armies launched "punitive expeditions" in the surrounding countryside, raping, butchering and pillaging at will. The American soldiers were ordered not to join the rampages. But they took part in their share of looting in Peking. And even some of the decent boys, who had been raised on the Golden Rule back home, forced themselves on Chinese girls.

As the allies' occupation of Peking dragged on, the soldiers' behavior grew more wanton. During a night of drunken revelry in the Palace of the Eighth Prince, where he and his fellow marine officers were quartered, Butler and his comrades sang raucous songs, smashed precious Buddha statues and drank themselves into oblivion. By then the marines encamped in the Forbidden City had "gone native," slipping on silk pantaloons and sashes as their ragged khakis fell to pieces, until they began looking like pirates. When a senior American officer arrived in Peking in September, he found the marines "demoralized" and "behaving badly," with the brig overflowing with looters and rapists.

Butler took offense at the "big rumpus kicked up" back in the United States over the soldiers' looting and lawlessness. "Some allowance should be made for the fact that during the excitement of a campaign you do things that you yourself would be the first to criticize in the tranquil security of home," he later wrote of the China expedition.

But, in his heart, Butler knew that some kind of sickness had settled into him and his troops during their Peking expedition. When the marines finally pulled out in October, as the weather was turning wet and dismal, Butler's malaise turned physical. Two days after his troop ship sailed for Manila, the young lieutenant was felled by typhoid fever, and he spent the rest of the sea journey confined to sick quarters, in the grip of delirium. Burning with fever, Butler hallucinated about China, reliving the ghastly trek from Tientsin and the rape of Peking. He envisioned his own death, dreaming that he and two fellow marines were marching down into the underworld. But while his comrades crossed over the shadowy River Styx to the other side, Butler chose not to.

When at last he emerged from his fever dream, Butler weighed only 90 pounds. But he was alive. And something had been purged from his soul. He had felt death and never again would he fear it.

CAPT. BUTLER TAKES A BRIDE TO-MORROW

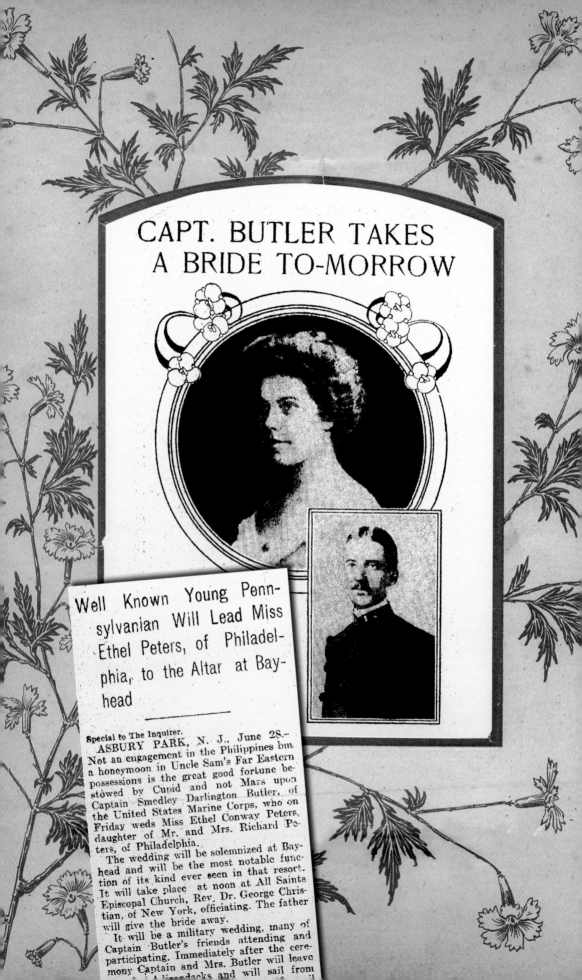

Well Known Young Pennsylvanian Will Lead Miss Ethel Peters, of Philadelphia, to the Altar at Bayhead

Special to The Inquirer.

ASBURY PARK, N. J., June 28.— Not an engagement in the Philippines but a honeymoon in Uncle Sam's Far Eastern possessions is the great good fortune bestowed by Cupid and not Mars upon Captain Smedley Darlington Butler, of the United States Marine Corps, who on Friday weds Miss Ethel Conway Peters, daughter of Mr. and Mrs. Richard Peters, of Philadelphia.

The wedding will be solemnized at Bayhead and will be the most notable function of its kind ever seen in that resort. It will take place at noon at All Saints Episcopal Church, Rev. Dr. George Christian, of New York, officiating. The father will give the bride away.

It will be a military wedding, many of Captain Butler's friends attending and participating. Immediately after the ceremony Captain and Mrs. Butler will leave

Act 2

TROPICAL FEVER

By the time Smedley Butler was 23, he was a veteran of three wars and a decorated marine captain. He had traveled the world and seen more than most men had in a lifetime. President Theodore Roosevelt called him "the ideal American soldier"—an impressive encomium from a man who valued the warrior ethic above all else.

And yet, young Butler knew that his life had not fully begun.

In the summer of 1904, Captain Butler found himself back in his hometown, in charge of a marine guard at the Philadelphia Navy Yard. It was lazy, aimless duty for a man of action, and the days drifted by slowly. Then he met Ethel Conway Peters.

She was the sister of an old prep school mate, Richard Peters, 3rd, who took Butler home to his family one day after bumping into him. The Peters family was Philadelphia royalty, with roots stretching back to the Colonial era. One ancestor managed the finances of the Revolutionary War and entertained George Washington, Thomas Jefferson and John Adams in his Philadelphia mansion. Ethel's mother also came from illustrious American stock: her father, railroad tycoon Samuel Felton, thwarted an assassination plot against Abraham Lincoln as the newly elected president rode from Springfield, Illinois, to Washington, D.C., and later ran the only railroad link between the nation's capital and Union troops.

The society pages chronicled the comings and goings of young Ethel and her parents as they yachted with the Astors or took lunch at the Newport Golf Club with the Vanderbilts or watched automobile parades alongside the Sedgwicks and the Goulds.

But, like Smedley, Ethel had managed to come of age in her Philadelphia blue-blood family without taking on any airs. She was a beautiful society belle. But her nose did not point upwards, and her feet were planted firmly on the ground.

Captain Butler was swept away. For the rest of the summer and into the fall, he laid siege to Ethel Peters, calling on her family at their Philadelphia home and their summer cottage on the Jersey shore.

He was so jarringly different from the other young Philadelphia gentlemen who came calling. He had none of their education or smooth manners. Yet she felt herself giving in to the lean, tattooed soldier, a man who looked ready for battle even in his dress blues. He carried with him the rough scent of faraway places. She imagined him in the heat of battle. She imagined him taking his pleasure with girls in waterfront bars. But he no longer wanted those girls…he wanted her. He wanted *her*. Soon they had developed a secret code, with numbers standing in for the moments of passion that they relived over and over when they were apart.

The young warrior emptied his heart to Ethel. "You are the first girl I have ever loved," he wrote to her. "I have always looked on such things, and on life in general, as a joke, but you have changed my ideas entirely."

After their visits, he was frantic with lust and longing. As soon as he returned to his barracks in the Navy Yard, he would throw himself into physical activity, bloodying himself in boxing bouts and football matches with his fellow marines. But he could not stop thinking about her.

"My precious Darling," he wrote, "when I left thee on the train this morning, I felt as if my insides were fastened to the last car and I still feel empty. Why on earth didn't we have a last kiss before leaving the house. I am crazy to hug thee again.

"Sweetheart, I love thee madly, blindly, passionately. I adore thee, Darling, worship

thee more than everything and all things on earth put together, and from my feeling of loneliness, more than any man could have loved a woman."

TEDDY ROOSEVELT (CENTER) VISITED THE **PANAMA CANAL** DIG.

The young officer and the society belle had found what they wanted, and nothing was going to stop them. When they were wed in June 1905 at the Peters's seaside retreat, it was the social event of the season. The newlyweds were toasted by the Eastern seaboard's finest families and saluted by a troop of marines in full dress uniform. But Ethel Peters Butler was not setting out on the same petal-strewn path as her sisters and cousins. Life with her new husband would be filled with rigors she never dreamed of as a young debutante.

He would take her and their children to the sun-scorched outposts of the American Empire. She would kiss him farewell time after time, never knowing whether she would ever feel his lips again. They would live from paycheck to paycheck. Her husband would sacrifice comfort for a life of service and turmoil. She would never again know the idle days of croquet on summer lawns. But she never flinched from their

EL TENIENTE RODRIGUEZ EN LAS EXCLUSAS DE GATUN, CANAL DE PANAMA.

⸱O BOAT "TENIENTE RODRIGUEZ" IN GATUN LOCKS, PANAMA CANAL   FEN-02

life together. Like him, she was made of that mettle that grew stronger under the hammer. They would march through life together, soldiers of the heart.

CAMP ELLIOTT, PANAMA, 1910

The Panama Canal Zone was no place for a young family. But that's where Major Smedley Butler brought his growing brood—including his wife, whom he now called "Bunny," three-year-old Ethel (or "Snooks") and baby Smedley, Jr.—when he was given command of the marine guard there. The canal was still under

construction, a massive gash through the jungle and rock overseen by army engineers and harnessing the sweat and muscle of thousands of Caribbean, Spanish and Italian laborers. The workers battled hellish heat, torrential rain, snakes, ravenous insects and tropical pestilence. Thousands succumbed to malaria and yellow fever before army doctors finally drained the swamps and exterminated the mosquitoes.

Meanwhile, Butler's marines stood a listless watch over the churning operation, killing time in their off hours in the nearby shanty towns, whoring, drinking and getting into street brawls with the Panamanian police. U.S. officials tried to bring some civility to the tropical outpost, building baseball fields, billiard rooms and ice cream parlors and holding Saturday night dances at the Hotel Rivoli, where quinine dispensers on the tables offered prophylaxis against malaria. But, all in all, it was a dreary posting for Butler and his family.

In November 1910, the routine was broken by the arrival of President William Howard Taft, who steamed into the port of Colón aboard the USS *Tennessee* to inspect the engineering wonder that he hoped would secure his place in history. (It didn't—the honor would go to his flashier nemesis, Teddy Roosevelt, who had started the project.) One day, the president—with his walrus mustache and whale dimensions—loomed into view, arriving by train at Butler's base, Camp Elliott. Taft was immense and sweating

On Butler's Tracks in Nicaragua

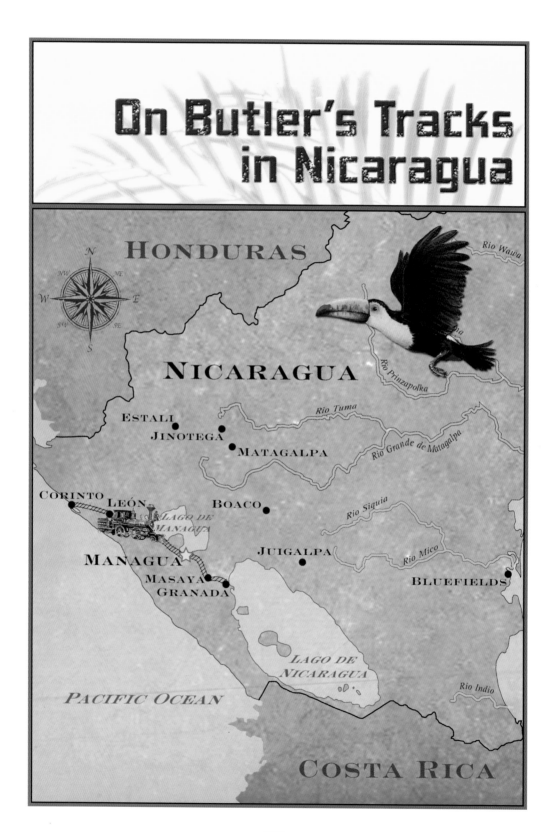

buckets in the tropical blaze, and his gout had flared up, forcing him off his aching feet. But Major Butler accomplished his own engineering feat, supervising the lifting of the enormous Taft into a creaking mule wagon, which then hauled the presidential load up a hill to the military parade ground.

Butler spent a pleasant afternoon with the president, reviewing the troops, chatting about the major's eminent father and Republican politics, and lunching on sandwiches and lemonade. "The president held my two babies, Snooks and Smedley, on his lap—what there was of it," Butler recalled.

Taft was not happy as president, and when he was unhappy, his weight ballooned to well over 300 pounds. TR had handpicked Taft to succeed him in the White House, after he had loyally served Roosevelt as his imperial proconsul in the Philippines and as his secretary of war. But after Roosevelt decided he wanted the presidency back, he made Taft's life hell. TR would run against him in 1912 on the Bull Moose ticket, dashing both of their presidential careers and handing the White House to Woodrow Wilson. Taft's aides sometimes found the big man in tears. Politics broke his heart.

But Taft loved to roam the world. And during the presidential trip to Panama, Major Butler found him "a simple, lovable man, with a delightful gift for putting folks at ease." As the afternoon waned, the giant figure leaned over to his uniformed host and confessed that he didn't want to return to Washington.

But Taft did return, weathering a violent sea storm off Cuba (even *that* he found enjoyable compared to the cutthroat politics awaiting him back home). Once back in the White House, he pursued an interventionist policy in the Caribbean basin that again would put Butler and his men in the line of fire. Taft insisted that his foreign policy substituted

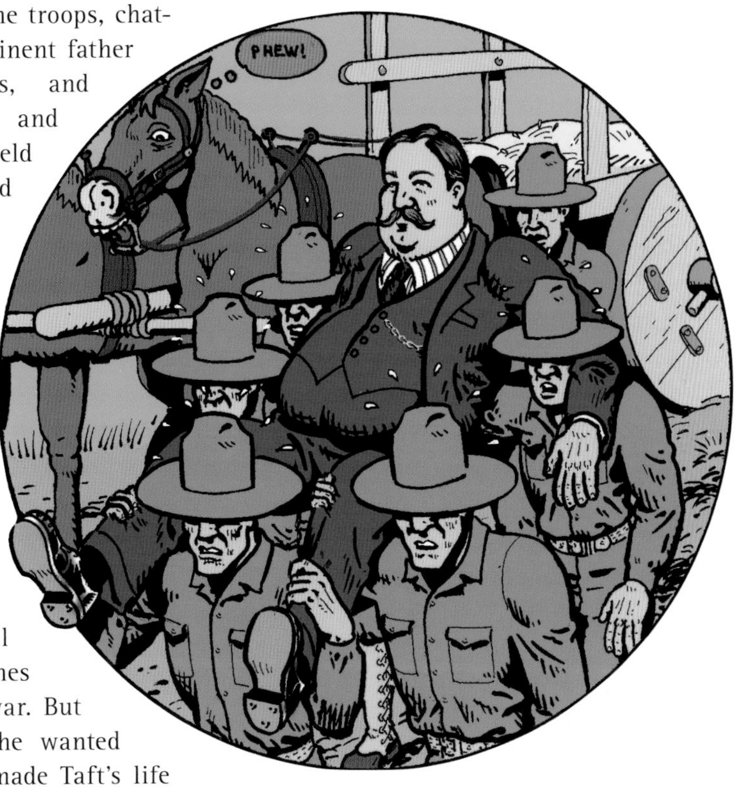
PHEW!

dollars for bullets—"dollar diplomacy," he called it. He said his policy was an enlightened step forward from the antics of his bully-boy predecessor, who was forever waving his "big stick" at our neighbors. But it turned out that foreign nations resented America's financial domination just as much as they did its military boot—and, in the end, the genial giant Taft would send American marines crashing ashore in the Caribbean more often than the Rough Rider himself. And when they went into battle, Major Smedley Butler was often leading the charge.

Panama would become the jumping-off platform for numerous U.S. Marine Corps forays into the banana republics, including Honduras, Mexico and—most of all—Nicaragua. Butler would grow drearily familiar with "the infernal hell hole" of Corinto, the squalid port town that was the American entryway to Nicaragua.

Nicaragua, August 1912

The train pulled out of Managua at midnight, with Major Butler riding shotgun in the locomotive and 100 marines and sailors under his command. It chugged slowly up the steep track, leaving Nicaragua's capital city—and the immense crater lake that it bordered—gleaming in the shadows below. Butler and his troops were headed for the port of Corinto, some 60 miles away, where they were to greet U.S. reinforcements. But their principal mission was to run a gauntlet of armed and angry rebels, and break the rail blockade that was strangling the capital. If the capital fell, so would the U.S.-backed regime.

So began the expedition that would make Smedley Butler a marine legend.

Huddled in a boxcar in the rear of the train was Commander Warren Terhune, the ranking U.S. officer in Nicaragua. Terhune had tried to run the blockade the week before with some of the same soldiers. But when a mob—including shouting, machete-wielding women—surrounded Terhune's train in the rebel stronghold of León, his nerve had failed him. The shaken naval commander surrendered his train to the rebels, who promptly stripped it of its American flag, and he and his humiliated troops were forced to straggle back to Managua in a pouring rain—earning Terhune the scathing nickname "General Walkemback."

Butler was outraged by the incident, which he called "the weakest piece of business I have ever heard of" in a letter to his parents in Philadelphia, adding that it made the American forces in Nicaragua "a laughingstock." Butler stormed into the hospital where the quivering Terhune had promptly checked himself in upon returning to Managua. The naval commander's higher rank did not intimidate the young major—Terhune had shamed the United States Marine Corps, and Butler was not going to let it stand. A fuming Butler found the commander reclining in his hospital bed, decked out in blue silk pajamas and

BUTLER, FAR RIGHT, AND JOHN LEJEUNE, SECOND RIGHT, BECAME MARINE LEGENDS IN THE BANANA WARS.

fortifying himself with periodic infusions of Scotch. Butler railed at him, demanding that he get to his feet and break the rebel blockade.

Terhune finally agreed, but he insisted that a horse be brought on the train, so he would not be forced to make the long trek back to Managua on foot if the rebels again humiliated him.

"If you come back, it will be feet first this time," the young major snarled at him.

Now the troop train was again entering rebel territory, and Terhune was only too happy to have Butler leading the charge this time, while he hunkered nervously in a rear car.

"I am going all the way to Corinto or 'bust,'" Butler had written to Ethel before leaving Managua. "If anything *should* happen to me, bring my Blessed Son up with the firm idea in his head that his Dadda was not a coward— whatever else he was (I mean hot tempered and profane at times), also my precious Nooksie [Snooks]."

The train made slow progress, repeatedly grinding to a halt where the rebels had torn up the tracks. As his men repaired the damage, Butler eyed the surrounding brush with his hand locked on his revolver. There was no sign of trouble until the train approached a trestle bridge outside León. At the opposite end of the bridge, a large rebel force had blocked the track with heavy rocks and were brandishing guns and flags.

RAILROADS WERE THE BATTLEGROUND.

When the rebels heard that the timorous "General Walkemback" was on the train, they began taunting him with catcalls. Terhune began to come undone again. He sent for Butler.

"We'd better surrender the train at once or we'll all be killed."

Butler was disgusted. "We'll do no such damned thing."

Instead, Butler began to walk across the bridge toward the blockade, accompanied by one of his lieutenants, E. H. Conger. Fearing that the rebels had sabotaged the bridge so it would collapse under the weight of the train, the two marines began to test its strength by crawling over the side of the bridge to inspect its underpinnings and trying not to look down at the deep ravine below.

When Butler and Conger reached the other side of the bridge, they were instantly confronted by the armed and agitated rebel soldiers, who ordered the Americans to reboard their train and go back to Managua. Butler just laughed. Conger tried diplomacy. He told them the marines did not want bloodshed. "We are simply opening the railroad, which we have a right to do, because it is American property." Now it was the rebels' turn to laugh. The Americans thought they owned everything.

The rebels—a ragtag army of peasants— were screaming in Spanish and waving their weapons, which ranged from rifles to razors. Conger tried to translate for Butler,

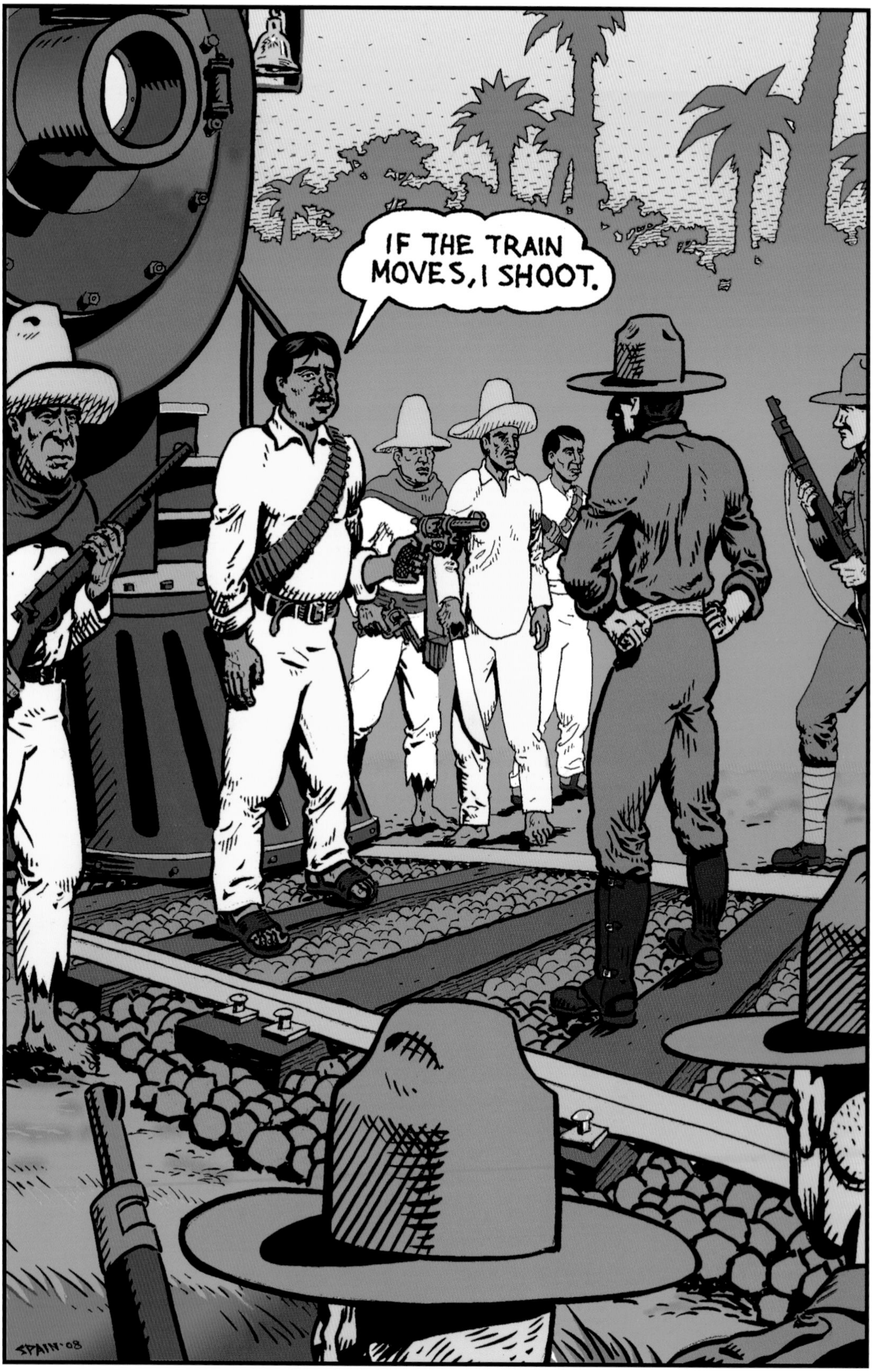
IF THE TRAIN MOVES, I SHOOT.
SPAIN·08

but the situation was quickly spiraling out of control. The two men were ringed by at least a thousand angry rebels. Meanwhile, on board the train, dozens of marines, jaws tensed, stood in the boxcar openings and on the platform cars, gingerly cradling their Springfield rifles and positioning their Gatling guns.

Just then, the rebel leader came running towards Butler. The marines on the train fingered their triggers. The rebel commander wore a bandolier across his chest and had a pistol shoved in his belt. He was full of swagger. He stuck his face menacingly in Butler's, but the marine didn't flinch. "I'm going on to Corinto," Butler informed him. "Now what are you going to do about it?"

In the blink of an eye, the rebel leader yanked the gun from his belt and stuck it in Butler's gut. "If the train moves," he told Butler, "I shoot."

The world stopped. Butler could not hear a sound. But he could see everything around him with the clarity of a hawk. "One hundred red-blooded Americans were clustered around the locomotive to see what I would do." If he backed down, he would humiliate his beloved Marine Corps. "If I signaled to the marines to shoot, there would be a frightful slaughter."

In a flash, Butler made a grab for the rebel's gun, snatching it from the shocked man's grip. Then, for a theatrical flourish, the marine emptied the cartridges onto the ground. There was a stunned silence. And, suddenly, hundreds of men—Nicaraguans and Americans—all burst into wild laughter. The death spell had been broken.

Butler succeeded in reaching Corinto, where he met with the commander of the Pacific fleet, Admiral William Southerland, who was assuming charge of the Nicaragua operation. Then, after taking on a couple hundred more sailors from battleships anchored in the harbor, Butler turned his train around and headed back to Managua.

The most hair-raising moment of Butler's return trip came on the sharp descent into the capital. The train had climbed some 1,500 feet to the peak of the volcanic mountains surrounding the capital, passing through coffee plantations and cloud forests. The sailors, fresh off the boat, marveled at the lush scenery of the Nicaragua highlands, including beds of lavender and gold orchids and canopy trees filled with circus-colored toucans and parrots. Steaming lava pools and smoking fissures in the rocks made clear that the lunar terrain was still not finished.

At the pinnacle, with the city shimmering far below, the train engineer informed Butler that their brakes were failing. Butler, still buzzing from his high-wire confrontations with the rebels, decided the fates were with him and ordered the engineer to take the plunge. The daredevil marine put two flat cars in front of the engine to absorb the collision in case the train hit another patch of torn-up track. Then he and an equally brash junior officer, Jim Vandegrift, jumped on the lead flat car and the train began hurtling downward.

By now it was dark and a steady drizzle was falling. The lights on the engine were out, and the only illumination came from a feeble lantern held aloft by a young sergeant. As the train picked up speed, rocketing downward into the gloomy unknown, the sergeant frantically waved his lantern in search of cows or boulders on the track. The sailors and marines, most of whom were packed into a boxcar in the rear, stared with wide-eyed terror into the pitch-black void. "Look out!" they yelled in unison as their bullet-train tilted madly into the curves.

By the time they hit the outskirts of Managua, the train was soaring so fast that it flew right past the government's army outposts. Startled sentries blazed fire at the speeding target, not knowing if it was friend or foe, but fortunately their aim was so haphazard that none of Butler's men were hit. The American ambassador and a boisterous crowd were gathered at the railroad station to greet Butler and his troops. But the train raced by them, stopping only when it struck an upgrade, after which it drifted slowly backwards to the waiting, dumbfounded delegation.

Afterward, Butler gave Vandegrift the nickname "Sunny Jim" because of the frozen grin pasted on the young lieutenant's face throughout their screeching descent into Managua. Sunny Jim Vandegrift would display his celebrated grit years later as the Marine Corps' commanding general at Guadalcanal.

THE CARIBBEAN WARS LOOKED THRILLING IN MARINE POSTERS.

As for Butler, he had dropped ten pounds on his harrowing, blockade-running trip. He estimated that he had slept no more than 17 hours during the entire week. But, he wrote home, it was both the most strenuous and the most exhilarating experience in his military career since the Boxer campaign. Days later, the U.S. consul in Corinto wired that "the backbone of the [rebel] uprising appears broken by opening railroad."

Soldiers want to fight for a just cause. They want to believe that there is a higher purpose to their sacrifice. President Taft, who sent the marines into Nicaragua on three separate occasions, claimed the United States was fighting to protect democracy and the lives of its citizens abroad. Major Butler knew better.

The press called these little invasions "banana wars"—but the marines' Nicaragua incursion was about Wall Street, not fruit. When José Santos Zelaya, Nicaragua's longtime Liberal president, began flexing his muscles—threatening to build his own Pacific-Atlantic canal with European aid and steadfastly refusing Wall Street loans to keep his country out of debt—the United States moved against him. Zelaya was forced out of office and replaced by Conservative Party oligarchs, who opened Nicaragua to American banking interests, which promptly took over the country's ports, railroads, mines and finances. Democracy was canceled, with Thomas Dawson, the U.S. envoy to Nicaragua, announcing that elections were "at present impracticable and dangerous to peace."

It was a cozy operation. The U.S. State Department was a virtual subsidiary of powerful investment banks like Brown Brothers. President Taft's secretary of state was a well-connected corporate lawyer named Philander Knox, who owned a piece of Nicaragua's major mining company, La Luz. Under Knox, the State Department agitated for a militant policy against Nicaraguan sovereignty, pushing a reluctant War Department into action. Meanwhile, the longtime bookkeeper of La Luz, Adolpho Díaz, was installed as Nicaragua's Conservative president, and Luis Mena, a major shareholder in the U.S.-controlled company, was named his top general.

Smedley Butler had been schooled by his father in the ways of Washington, and none of this was lost on him. The more he learned about the mercantile reasons for U.S. intervention in Nicaragua, the more disgusted he became. "This is not, by any means, my first experience wielding the 'Big Stick' in shady diplomacy, but it is the most sickening," Butler wrote his father after his first foray into Nicaragua, to help overthrow Nicaragua's Liberal government. "The whole attitude of our State Department is beyond me, but of course I am simply a

hired policeman and am not supposed to understand affairs of state." But even with his "untrained eyes," added Butler sarcastically, he could see how rotten a scheme it was. And his marines were paying for it with their blood.

Despite his growing distress about his mission, Butler was a soldier and he obeyed his orders. And, in late September, after successfully retaking Nicaragua's railroads, the marine major was ordered to force the surrender of the rebels' dashing leader—none other than General Luis Mena.

Mena had helped topple the Liberal government and he had served as Conservative president Díaz's military commander. As U.S. financial interests took over Nicaragua's economy, Mena had been cut in on his share of the spoils. But at some

IN A CARTOON OF THE DAY, A MARINE BULLDOG SCARES OFF A NATIVE.

POETRY OF FIRE

After Nicaragua fell under Yankee sway, the country's independent spirit was kept alive by rebels of the heart like celebrated poet Rubén Darío. Leader of the Modernistas, a Latin American aesthetic movement that sought its own voice, apart from the old empire of Spain and the new empire to the north, Darío was a dashing globe-trotting figure as comfortable in bohemian salons as in government ministries. Named envoy to Spain by Nicaragua's Liberal president José Santos Zelaya, Darío remained loyal to the deposed leader after he was ousted by the United States, staying with Zelaya for a time during his Barcelona exile. Darío's resentment of Washington's big-stick domination burst into flame in his poem "To Roosevelt"—the man whom he believed personified the American colossus.

Darío's poem includes these scorching words:

*You think that life is a fire,
that progress is an eruption,
that the future is wherever
your bullet strikes.*

No.

…

*O men with Saxon eyes and
barbarous souls,
our America lives. And dreams.
And loves.
And it is the daughter of the Sun. Be careful.
Long live Spanish America!
A thousand cubs of the Spanish lion are
roaming free.
Roosevelt, you must become, by God's own will,
the deadly Rifleman and the dreadful Hunter
before you can clutch us in your iron claws.*

*And though you have everything, you are
lacking one thing:
God!*

point, the increasing humiliation of his native country became too much for Mena. He decided to become a patriot again and take up arms against his fellow Conservatives, who had sold out their country.

Mena's former allies in the Nicaraguan oligarchy heaped scorn on him. The aristocratic families in Granada, his hometown, had never fully welcomed the man they regarded as a "semisavage Indian" into their exclusive circle. Now they vowed to destroy him. But Nicaragua's Liberal press hailed Mena's transformation. Newspapers said the 47-year-old mestizo was returning to his roots as a man of the people. Rubén Darío, the celebrated Nicaraguan poet, heralded him as a "rustic and awesome general…a man of the machete and of popular values."

Butler remembered Mena. He had met him a couple of years before when he was fighting for the Conservatives. Butler thought well of him. He recalled him as a simple man. "He had been an ox driver, a rough giant of a man with great physical strength and vitality." But now Butler's job was to track him down and destroy him. In the end, the marine officer would end up "hat[ing] my job like the Devil."

Just before Butler and his troops were to pull out of Managua for Granada, where General Mena and the main rebel force were dug in, the major was stricken with a bout of malaria—a recurring scourge during his duty in the tropics. For days, Butler suffered miserably in bed, burning up with a 104-degree fever and soaking his sheets. He subsisted on quinine and limeade. Finally, fearing the expedition would leave without him, he dragged himself out of bed and slipped some ice in his mouth to reduce his temperature, so the doctor would pronounce him fit for service.

"Everything swam around me and my knees crumpled like paper, but I managed to get to the train, where I lay on a cot in a box car," Butler recalled. "I wasn't strong enough to stand up.

"We creaked along asthmatically from Managua toward Granada. Every jolt stabbed through me. Of course I was an idiot to go, but nothing short of chains could have held me back."

From time to time, the train ground to a halt, wheels spinning, where rebels had soaped the tracks, and Butler's 400 marines were forced to get out and push from behind. Finally, as night fell, they reached Masaya, 15 miles from the capital, a town ringed by hills that were under rebel control.

The train rumbled slowly down a narrow street. The town was as black and silent as a tomb; not one light shined in a window. Butler was taking the night air on the lead flat car, sitting next to a sergeant who held aloft a lantern. Suddenly, by their weak light, they saw a man gallop by on a horse. The horseman turned and fired directly into their faces, narrowly missing Butler and wounding a soldier directly behind him. Butler, still wobbly and ill, jumped off the car to give chase. As he shuffled weakly down the train embankment, he came to an abrupt stop. Peering into the murky distance, he realized the train was drifting directly into an ambush. Ahead, the man on the white steed was urging 150 horsemen to attack.

Suddenly, the night erupted in flames, with bullets zinging everywhere. Rifles were blazing at the train from every darkened window. Butler ordered his men to open fire and jumped into the fireman's

GEN. MENA WAS NOW BUTLER'S ENEMY.

seat for cover. The marines began pumping away with the 16 machine guns mounted along the top of the train. All of Butler's drowsy malaise immediately drained out of him. The battle-hardened marine was fully in charge, barking orders at his soldiers and thrilling to the urgency of the moment. "It was a gorgeous spectacle." That's the way he would later describe this brush with death.

When the firefight finally stopped, dozens of rebels were sprawled along the track. Butler ordered the train forward, and after it rattled safely out of town, he stopped to check his losses. He was surprised to find only four of his men had been wounded, and none killed. Now Butler was more determined than ever to complete his mission.

A short distance from Granada, the marines stopped to repair a final stretch of torn-up track and Butler sent a messenger ahead to inform General Mena that the U.S. military was about to descend on him. If Mena didn't interfere with his troops, there would be no fighting. When Mena responded by sending a delegation to meet with Butler, the major packed his 400 men tightly around him in a semicircle to appear like he was leading a force of thousands. The trick worked. A rattled Mena sent Butler a letter, promising to relinquish all sections of the railroad still under his control and to grant American troops safe passage through rebel territory.

Butler met with Admiral Southerland, who had arrived from Managua, to plot his next move. By then, the major had

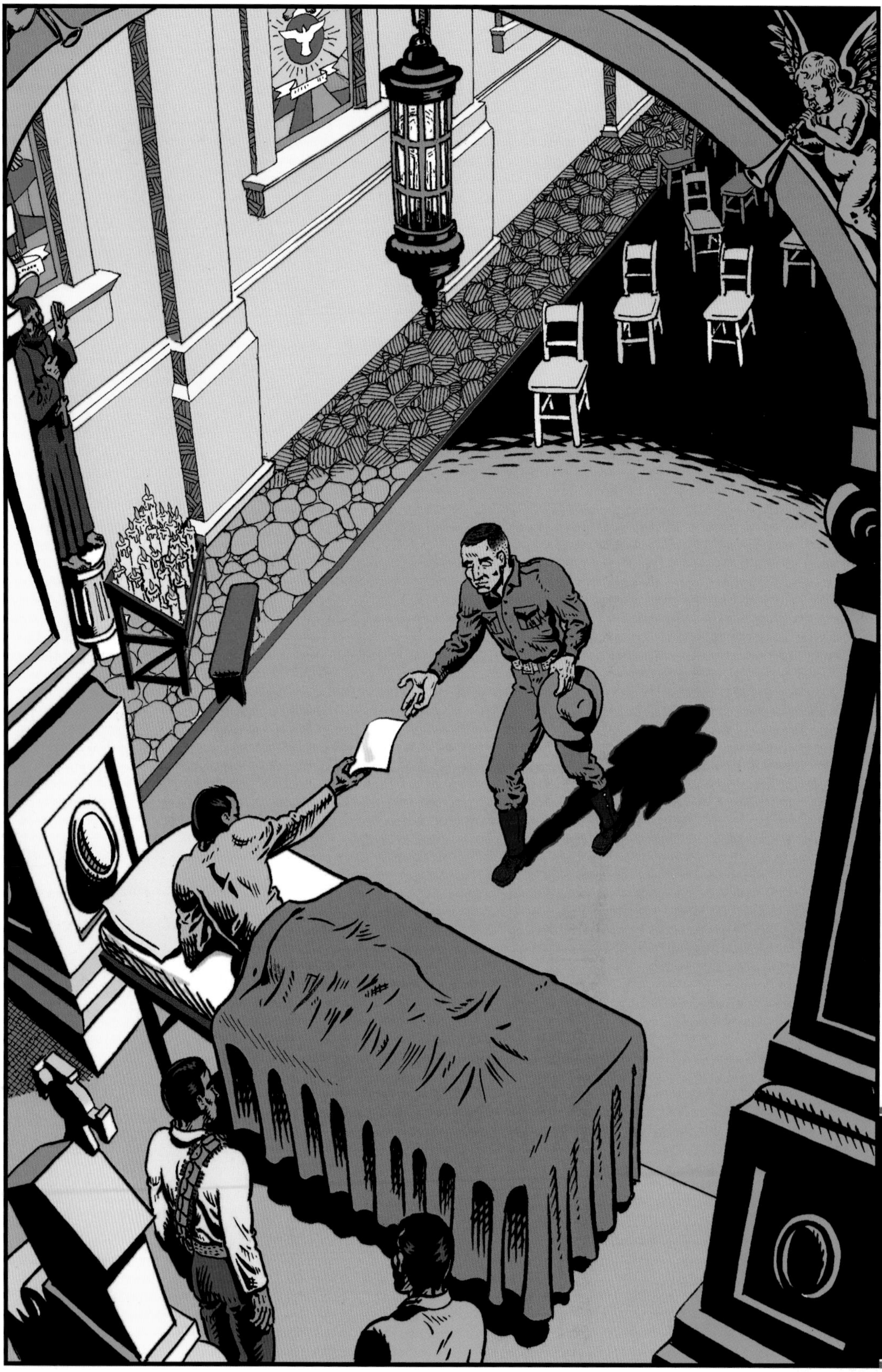

marched his marines into Granada, pitching camp in a plaza in front of the railroad station. Now that he had reached Mena's doorstep, Butler was eager to press his advantage. When Southerland asked him what he wanted to do next, he quickly replied, "Admiral, I'm in favor of getting Mena to surrender and throw himself on your mercy, and then have him sent on an American ship to Panama."

That night, Butler mulled over how he could accomplish this delicate task. There was only one way, he decided. He would walk directly into Mena's stronghold, without any soldiers, and speak man to man with the rebel general. It was midnight, and he was still dizzy from his malarial crisis, but the marine seized the moment. He struck out for the colonial-era cathedral where Mena and his troops were barricaded, moving unsteadily through the city's dusty streets.

"The moon was in the last quarter," Butler recalled, "and it was gruesome walking through the dark, deserted streets past ghostly white houses half hidden behind thick screens of rustling trees."

At last he came upon the San Francisco Cathedral, which Mena had made his headquarters. By day it was a festive-looking edifice, with its Caribbean-blue adobe walls and white columns and cornices. But in the dark, it loomed like a gothic fortress. Butler walked up the stone steps, knocked on a gate in the annex and announced to the startled sentry he was there to see General Mena. The guard quickly returned with Daniel Mena, the general's son and aide, who led Butler inside.

Butler followed the general's son into the cavernous cathedral. It was an eerie scene. The cathedral was cloaked in shadows, lit only by two old lanterns, which hung by long ropes from the dome. In the distance, Butler could hear a terrible moaning, and at first he thought it was the laments of the Granada aristocrats whom the rebels were said to be torturing in the basement of the cathedral. As they proceeded down the aisle, Butler detected the source of the ghastly sounds. "There on an old canvas cot, behind a gigantic stone arch lay Mena, the heart and soul of the rebellion," writhing in agony. "And all around on the stone floor, and on boxes and sandbags used in barricading the doors and windows, slept Mena's bodyguard, which, in the dim light, gave the place the appearance of a slaughter pen."

Daniel Mena told Butler that his father was suffering from Bright's Disease, an excruciating kidney affliction. Flushed and sweating from his own illness, the marine felt he had descended into the flames of hell. But he pulled himself together and walked over to Mena's bed, where he quietly greeted his old military ally.

Mena looked at Butler through his rheumy eyes and managed a weak smile. The two soldiers reminisced briefly about their days together in Bluefields, the old pirate port on Nicaragua's Caribbean coast where the U.S. marines had made their camp. But neither had energy for much talk. Butler quickly came to the point, laying out "the whole sad story." Mena had to surrender himself and all his men. If he did, Butler was sure that Admiral Southerland would show him mercy and grant him, as well as his son, safe passage to Panama. Mena knew he was in no condition to put up a fight, and he agreed to the deal.

Butler quickly returned to the little house where Admiral Southerland had set

> **Butler met with the sick general in a gloomy cathedral.**

THE LAST BULLET
THE REBELLION THAT WOULD NOT DIE

General Luis Mena, leader of Nicaragua's rebel army, would go down in history as a national disgrace for surrendering to Smedley Butler's smaller force. But Mena's top officer, Benjamin Zeledón, decided to keep fighting against the U.S. invaders. And his heroic stand would inspire future generations of Nicaraguan freedom fighters.

A week after Mena was shipped off to exile in Panama, Zeledón and a force of 800 rebels were surrounded by 1,000 American marines and 4,000 government troops outside Masaya. The marines—who were under the command of Butler and his superior officer, future military legend Colonel Joseph Pendleton—were in no mood to show Zeledón mercy. It was Zeledón's force that had ambushed Butler's train in Masaya just days earlier. Nonetheless, Pendleton did the honorable thing and offered Zeledón 24 hours to surrender.

The 33-year-old Zeledón had much to live for. The son of a carpenter, he had become a rising young lawyer, marrying into a wealthy Conservative family and fathering four children. Despite his new affluence, Zeledón was a patriot. When the marines landed, Zeledón took up arms against the invaders. Now, trapped on a hill-top, his hours seemed numbered.

His father-in-law, a prosperous coffee grower, was given permission to meet with Zeledón, to persuade him not to leave behind a widow and four fatherless children. A life of riches would be his if he gave up. Pendleton predicted that Zeledón would take the deal and come "crawling down."

But early the next morning, no white flags flew on the hilltop, and the marines prepared to storm the peak. Instead of a letter of surrender, the rebel leader sent down a defiant note, invoking Washington, Jefferson and Lincoln, and condemning "the Great Nation that prides itself on being the guiding spirit of liberty," for using its military might "against the weak." He vowed to fight "until the last cartridge."

Zeledón also wrote a letter to his wife, a final testament that would live on for years as a rallying cry for Nicaraguan sovereignty. "Your papa tried to convince me using all the arguments that his love and his rhetorical gifts could inspire. He talked to me of the duty that I have to save my life to protect yours and that of our little children, those pieces of my heart for whom I want there to be a free and sovereign Nicaragua. But we couldn't agree, because while he was thinking of the family, I was thinking of the patria, that is, the mother of all Nicaraguans… If I die, don't cry, because I will always accompany you in spirit."

Soon after, Butler and Pendleton charged up the hill with their troops and overran Zeledón's trenches. The rebel leader managed to escape with a small band, but they were quickly captured by government troops, who killed Zeledón. Government horsemen then dragged the fallen rebel's body through the streets of local villages, as a warning to those who might join future rebellions.

This macabre display had a profound effect on one young villager that day, a 17-year-old boy named Augusto Sandino. It did not weaken his resolve—it made him want to fight back. Years later, he vowed to pick up "the stone"—the freedom struggle—that Zeledón once carried. And when Sandino too was cut down, a new generation of liberation fighters named in his honor—the Sandinistas—would carry on.

Zeledon is commemorated on currency; Sandino carries on the legacy.

50

up his headquarters, waking him up to tell him the good news. They opened cans of cold salmon and apricots to celebrate.

Butler finally collapsed into bed after 3 a.m. But at 5:45 he was shaken awake by the admiral's orderly, who told him the naval commander needed to see him immediately. He threw on his uniform and hustled back to see Southerland, who greeted Butler grimly with a cablegram in his hand. The admiral had just received orders from Washington to arrest General Mena and turn him over to the Conservative government in Managua—which would mean the rebel leader's certain death.

Butler fell backwards into a chair as if he had been clubbed. His word meant everything to him. But now he was being ordered by Washington—which undoubtedly meant the bloodthirsty bankers in the State Department—to betray the noble foe with whom he had just made a solemn pact.

Southerland was also heartsick. It violated his sense of honor too. He couldn't do it. The admiral patted Butler's shoulder. "Don't worry, Butler, I'll stick by you." He immediately cabled the War Department, informing navy officials that the arrest order had come too late; Mena was already leaving the country.

That night, Butler stood watch as a marine escort entered the dark cathedral, lifted the suffering general onto a stretcher and gently carried him onto a train to Corinto, where he would safely board a ship to Panama. Mena was supposed to be his enemy. But, watching the frail and wasted form of the once brawny soldier being carried down the empty streets of Granada, Butler felt the occasion was as melancholy as a funeral. "In fact, it was a funeral—of the man's hopes," Butler reflected.

Where was the joy in this kind of victory?

Not long after Mena's surrender, Butler's marines overpowered the final rebel outpost. Nicaragua was now firmly in control of the empire to the north and its docile accomplices in the Conservative regime. The Brown Brothers office in Managua announced it was throwing a party to celebrate the defeat of the rebels. Major Smedley Butler and his fellow officers were to be the bankers' guests of honor. But the popular mood in the capital city was bleak. People could not understand why their hero, General Mena, had surrendered to the marines, when his own forces vastly outnumbered those of Butler.

At the party, Butler found it hard to get in a festive mood, despite the free-flowing rum punch and the effusive toasts to his courageous leadership. Portly bankers in white linen suits—and their tipsy and flirtatious wives—wanted to meet the man who had stared down the rebel army. One American woman cornered Butler and told him that he had a ferocious reputation among the Nicaraguan people. "Do you know," she said, looking queerly into his eyes, "how the locals talk of you? They call you a 'Walking Devil'...a regular fire eater."

Butler felt sick. He shouldn't have been drinking when he was still getting the sweats. He wanted to leave the party, to get as far away from these people as he could.

Butler poured out his feelings to his wife. This latest U.S. incursion had cost some 2,000 lives, including dozens of young marines, and what was it all about? "It is terrible that we should be losing so many men," he wrote her, "all because Brown Bros. have some money down here."

Smedley Butler was beginning to see the light. But darkness and mortal danger still lay ahead for him.

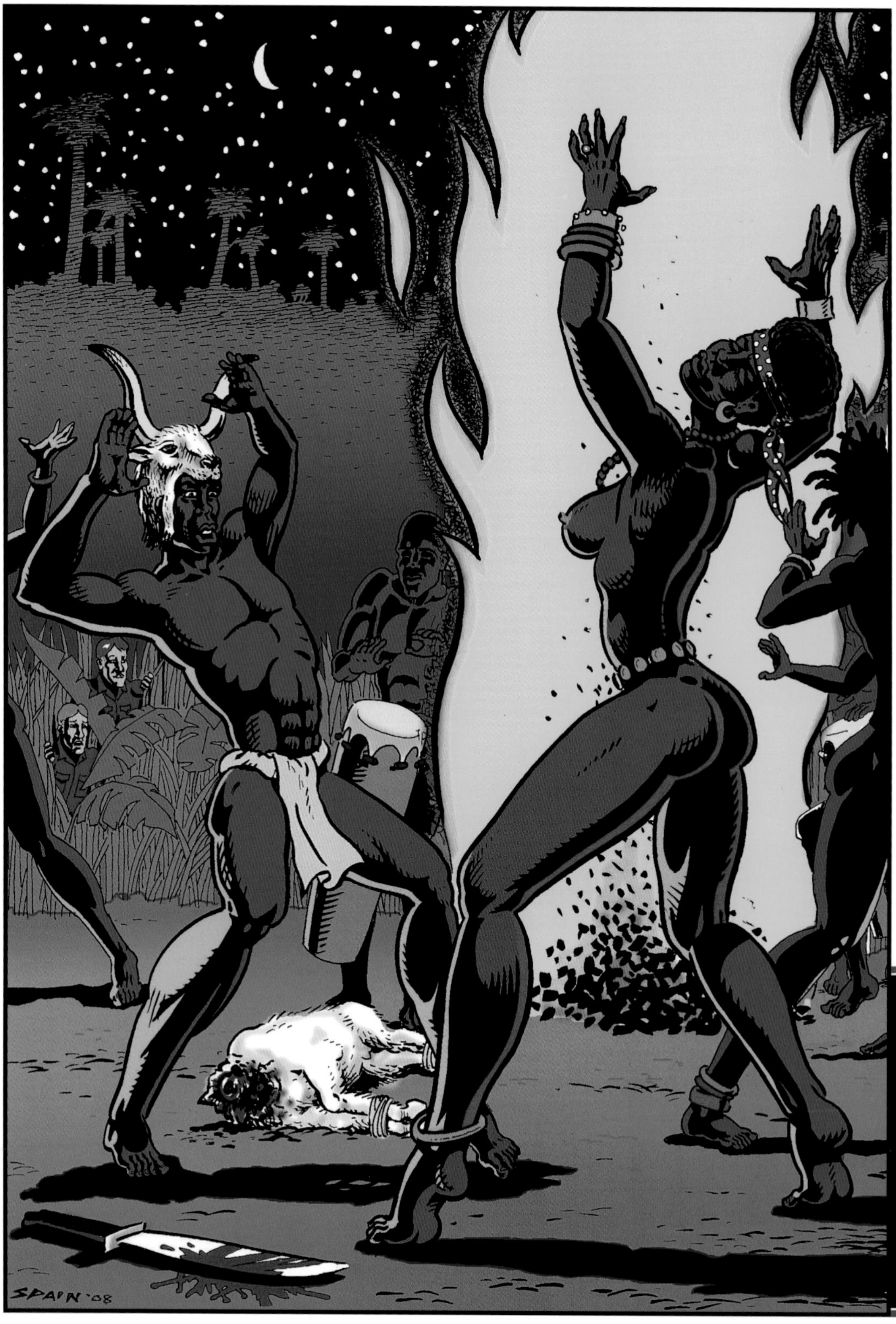
SPAIN '08

Act 3

LAND OF THE

LIVING DEAD

PORT-AU-PRINCE, JULY 1915

The scraggy street dogs began barking first. Then came the gunfire.

At the U.S. legation, where the early morning sun was seeping through the arcade windows, R. B. Davis, the dutiful chargé d'affaires, was rattled awake by the percussive noise. The shooting was coming from the direction of the presidential palace, and Davis quickly concluded that yet another Haitian government was in the process of being violently toppled.

President Jean Vilbrun Guillaume Sam, who had seized the palace a mere four months before, was indeed coming to the end of his brief and brutal reign. Sam was the latest in a long line of Haitian leaders whose presidencies were abruptly terminated. But his downfall was not only the most macabre—it had the most tragic effect on Haiti.

Because watching the bloody chaos unfold in Port-au-Prince from his armored cruiser on the horizon was Admiral William Banks Caperton of the United States Navy. And on their way to reinforce Admiral Caperton were troop ships carrying America's most feared colonial warriors, including marine legend Major Smedley Darlington Butler. And despite the stirring words that inevitably cascaded from Washington before men like this arrived on a distant shore, they were not bringing freedom and democracy, or even peace.

> **The marines tried to tame Haiti's wild spirit. But some soldiers went native.**

As the gunfire kept on through the day, increasingly gruesome reports drifted into the U.S. legation. President Sam—who had rounded up the young men of Port-au-Prince's elite, mulatto class as hostages to secure his rough-handed rule—was said to be abusing them behind bars. When his palace came under attack that morning, he scrambled over the high stone garden wall to seek refuge in the adjacent French legation. But, as he escaped, Sam sent word to his military enforcer to butcher all 200 of his political prisoners. Sam's henchmen dragged the captives from their cells and, slashing and hacking with every sharp blade that came to hand, turned the prison courtyard into a bog of blood.

> SAM'S **CRUEL** REIGN CAME TO A CRUEL **END.**

Davis, accustomed to more refined postings than the Haitian capital, could not believe the grisly stories. He plunged boldly into the city's riotous streets to find out what was really going on. As he made his way through the teeming thoroughfares, a terrible wail began echoing through the city, and he realized with a shiver that the stories were true. The diplomat came upon one wretched sight after the next. Weeping women were washing the torn and bloody bodies of their loved ones. "Is it you, my love, that I touch and hold?" sobbed one. Other families carried the dismembered remains of their sons and brothers in baskets toward the great church of the Sacred Heart.

That night, back in his residence, Davis received a frantic note from the French legation—they were having great difficulty keeping a mob from storming the grounds and forcibly taking President Sam, who was cowering with his family in their official quarters. Davis again took to the streets to lend the French minister his help, pushing his way through a mob gathered outside the legation. As Davis entered the walled grounds, he was greeted by his grateful French and British counterparts, who led him across the palm-studded lawn into the main residence. Inside was President Sam, surrounded by his wife and small children, and several of his ministers and military aides. Normally a regal-looking figure with a dapper mustache and a high, commanding forehead, Sam was now a broken man, limping around the legation mansion with a bandage wrapped around his posterior, where he had taken a bullet while hurtling over the garden wall. "The president himself was in a perfect frenzy of fear," observed Davis, "creeping about the house like a hunted animal, so terror stricken that when passing an open window he would crawl on all fours for fear some one on the outside would see him and shoot him."

The diplomats tried to keep the president safe, but as the full horror of the prison massacre swept through the city, the mob outside grew in size and fury. At last it could not be contained. Men and women wielding clubs and machetes and knives pushed their way past the French chargé d'affaires and began combing the rooms for President Sam, who had barricaded himself in a toilet. At first, they were unable to find him, but they knew he was wounded. And when someone smelled the sweetish scent of iodoform, the antiseptic dressing used on Sam's wound, he was given away.

"He was seized by the mob, stabbed two or three times in his face, knocked down and dragged by his heels down the stairs through the drawing room and out into the grounds, vainly protesting that he was innocent of any connection with the massacre of the day before, and begging most piteously for his life."

But his captors took as little pity on Sam as he had on their loved ones behind bars. When he grabbed on to the spokes of a buggy as he was being dragged along the ground, they loosened his grip by breaking his arm with a heavy, gold-headed cane. Then they hoisted him onto the legation wall and threw him like scrap meat to the snarling crowd below.

The intrepid Davis shoved his way through the mob to see if Sam could be rescued, but there was nothing he could do. "I could see that something or somebody was on the ground in the center of the crowd, just before the gates, and when a man disentangled himself from the crowd and rushed howling by me, with a severed hand from which the blood was dripping—the thumb of which he had stuck in his mouth—I knew that the threatened assassination of the president was accomplished. Behind him came men with the feet, the other hand, the head and other parts of the body displayed on poles, each one followed by a mob of screaming men and women. The portion of the body that remained was dragged through the streets by the crowd."

Such a carnival of gore! Many long-suffering Haitian people, sickened by this latest orgy of blood, dropped to their knees and begged for deliverance. A peasant woman flung out her arms like a crucifix and cried out, "They say that the white man is coming to rule Haiti again. The black man is so cruel to his own, let the white men come!"

It was an agony of a prayer. But when it came true, it was more like a curse.

A DEFIANT CACO: THESE RAGTAG REBELS BRAVELY FOUGHT THE U.S. OCCUPATION.

HAYTI, Port au Prince.

FROM THE SEA, HAITI LOOKED LIKE PARADISE. ON SHORE IT BECAME HELL.

Fairyland. That's what one young marine, a refugee from the coal mines of Pennsylvania, called it as Haiti loomed into view. As the ship sliced through the white-foamed, blue-green waters, the soldiers gathered on the bow felt like they were sailing into paradise. Ahead of them, purple mountains disappeared into a halo of shimmering clouds. Emerging from the peaks' shadows was an emerald-green valley dotted with gaily colored shanties that tumbled all the way down to the sea. Everything seemed bathed in a warm, celestial light. The marines were knights on a noble mission, coming to rescue a tragic people in a magical land. It was the adventure of a lifetime.

Then they landed, and the dream ended.

On shore, the raunchy stink of rotting fruit, bad fish and human waste assaulted the senses. The primitive look and feel of the place, and its rank poverty, were an offense to everything the marines held dear. They somehow blamed the people themselves for it. And the people…instead of greeting the soldiers as liberators, they lined the curbs of the narrow streets, staring blankly as the troops filed by. Their silence was tormenting. No one smiled, no one waved. Their black faces were stone masks.

What are we doing here? More than one miner's son and farm boy in Marine Corps khaki asked himself that question as he trudged through the streets of Port-au-Prince and Cap-Haitien.

Major Butler knew all too well by now why they were there. And it had nothing to do with President Wilson's pious rhetoric. Wilson had righteously proclaimed that "we do not want a foot of anybody's territory." His Latin American forays were motivated by higher ideals; we would uplift our less fortunate neighbors to the south, and eventually they would join the United States "upon those great heights where there shines, unobstructed, the light of the justice of God."

Butler didn't buy a word of it. Wilson could save it for the college kids at

Princeton, where he once presided. Or the editorial board of the *New York Times*. Those fellows lapped up that stuff. The occupation of Haiti was "not pleasant work," opined the *Times* men, "but it had to be done." Of course, there were skeptics who suggested that Caribbean expeditions like this had more to do with "Wall Street profits" than the desire to bring peace and prosperity to Haiti, but these "objections," the newspaper said, were "puerile."

From where Butler stood, in the muck and blood of America's colonial wars, it was newspapers like the *Times* that were naïve. The marines were being used in Haiti as "a glorified bill collecting agency," Butler groused. This time they were acting as musclemen for the National City Bank of New York, one of the principal loan sharks that kept Haiti permanently impoverished. City Bank had extended high-risk loans to Haitian officials desperate for capital. To secure the loans, the bank took over more and more of the country's economy, from farms to railroads. But the

big prize eluded City Bank: Haiti's customhouse, whose import and export fees provided the nation with its only major flow of cash. When the marines landed, Butler's men promptly took control of the customhouse, to the delight of Wilson's top Haiti advisor, a banker by the name of Roger L. Farnham.

It was Farnham who had relentlessly lobbied the Wilson administration to invade Haiti. The banker persuaded Wilson that if he did not intervene to restore order on the island, then Germany—a feared rival of U.S. interests in the Caribbean—would. Of course, when the marines did charge ashore, the main beneficiary of their bill collecting was none other than Farnham's employer—National City Bank—where he served as a vice president.

And so began the U.S. occupation of Haiti, which would drag on for nearly twenty years. The occupation would weigh heavily on the Haitian people, and eat away at the American soldiers who had to enforce it.

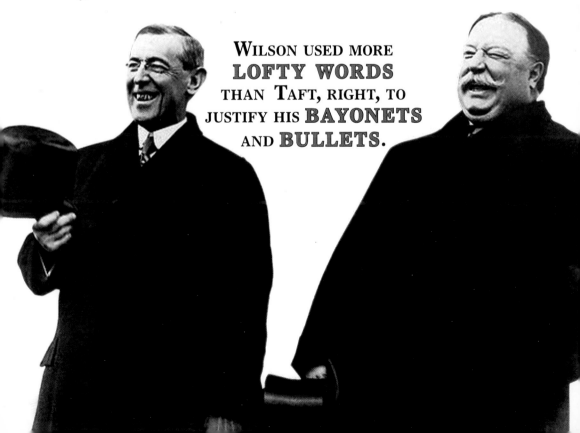

WILSON USED MORE LOFTY WORDS THAN TAFT, RIGHT, TO JUSTIFY HIS BAYONETS AND BULLETS.

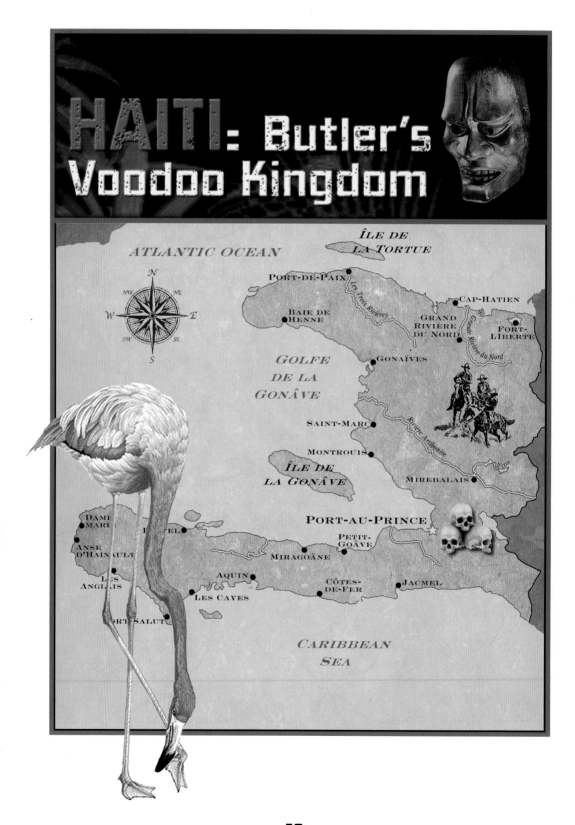

HAITI: Butler's Voodoo Kingdom

ÎLE DE LA TORTUE

ATLANTIC OCEAN

PORT-DE-PAIX

Les Trois Rivières

CAP-HATIEN

BAIE DE HENNE

GRAND RIVIÈRE DU NORD

Grande Rivière du Nord

FORT-LIBERTE

GOLFE DE LA GONÂVE

GONAÏVES

SAINT-MARC

Rivière Artibonite

MONTROUIS

ÎLE DE LA GONÂVE

MIREBALAIS

PORT-AU-PRINCE

DAME MARI

EL

PETIT-GOÂVE

ANSE D'HAINAULT

MIRAGOÂNE

LES ANGLAIS

AQUIN

CÔTES-DE-FER

JACMEL

LES CAYES

RT SALUT

CARIBBEAN SEA

In the steamy dime-store novels that became popular with American readers during the long occupation of Haiti—pulps like *Black Medicine*, *Voodoo* and *The Goat Without Horns*—white men lost their souls to bare-breasted African she-devils and the island's dark rhythms. Butler would lose part of his soul in Haiti, but not to black magic. He was in danger of becoming a cynical man, a man who knew he had become a hired gun and took out his rage on the people whose country he had invaded.

Many of the officers and rank-and-file marines in the Haiti expedition were white southerners, including the commander of the operation, Colonel Littleton Waller, Butler's old friend and patron going back to the Boxer Rebellion days. Waller came from an old plantation family; descendants of his were among the victims of Nat Turner's slave rebellion. Waller was a vicious racist, revolted by the very notion of a sovereign black nation. He found it repugnant to conduct business with the country's proud officials, whom he dismissed as "uppity" clowns.

Butler began slipping into the same coarse and sneering manner. He was furious to once again find himself cleaning up a tinpot nation's mess, and he spouted his fury at the Haitian elites who had allowed their country to descend into such bloody chaos. Haiti's political class was proud of its independent heritage, of how the nation was created by slaves who drove out their French masters and then defeated Napoleon's army when he tried to retake the island. Haiti, they reminded their American occupiers, was the second-oldest democracy in the Western hemisphere, after the United States itself.

All this fell on deaf ears with Butler. It was the abysmal failure of Haiti's leaders to govern peacefully that had brought him here. If they were going to act like savages, that is what he was going to call them,

despite their snooty French frock coats and accents.

In Nicaragua, he had developed a grudging respect for his rebel opponents. But in Haiti, he used the raw language of his fellow bush soldiers when talking about the enemy. He referred to the rebel Cacos by the vilest epithets—"bad niggers," "shaved apes." He ridiculed their struggle. He hated himself for running after them through the bush.

One afternoon, Butler found himself chasing after a rebel general named Rameau, who was threatening to burn the railroad outside Gonaïves, the coastal city where Haitian independence was declared in 1804. When he caught up with him, their encounter was brutal and comic. Butler asked several of his soldiers to begin shouting Rameau's name at the top of their lungs, and the rebel leader finally responded to the challenge, cantering over to Butler on his horse.

Rameau stared down at Butler. "He was a sour-looking, vicious little devil, and he screwed up his face maliciously as he looked down at me," Butler wrote. He told Rameau to get off his horse "and stand on the ground as I'm doing."

When Rameau responded by mumbling something derogatory about the United States, Butler reached up and jerked him out of his saddle. "This was more humiliating to him than defeat in battle," Butler later observed. "The horse episode really finished him, and he surrendered."

The truth is that the Cacos rebels stood up to Butler's marines again and again, even though they were so outnumbered and outgunned that to do so was certain death. Hunting the Cacos, Butler said, was like "hunting pigs."

The whole thing stunk. It was not the American way. But he continued to lead the "hunt and kill" missions, as the marines called their grim work. And he did so with a rage and abandon that would either get him killed or win him a medal.

Butler's next mission would take him into the mountains, the land of voodoo, and the heart of Haiti's reckless and brave resistance.

Butler set off from his base at Cap-Haitien with 27 soldiers on ponies, followed by a team of pack mules. Colonel Eli Cole, the commander of his regiment, said that it would take a full six battalions—3,000 men—to wipe out the Cacos in their mountain stronghold. Butler thought Cole worried too much—it came from being one of those "over-educated" officers. "I never went to any military school," Butler liked to say, "and so perhaps I wasn't trained to know danger when I saw it." All he needed, Butler told Cole, was a couple of dozen of the regiment's most battle-hardened men—his kind of marines. The ones who "did all the bush work and never had time to go to school."

Butler's grizzled crew rode up the rocky ravines for three straight days without pitching camp. They kept climbing, not stopping for sleep, to avoid giving the Cacos inviting targets. They tracked the rebels by following the orange peels they left behind; if the peels were still moist, Butler's men knew the enemy was close.

On the third night, a drizzling rain began to spatter the marine patrol as their ponies picked their way up a particularly steep canyon trail. Two hundred feet below, Butler could hear the roar of a cascading river. Just thinking about the drop into the black gorge made him dizzy. By now, Butler's mount—whom he had named Tom Dick, after his youngest son—was lame, his hoofs worn to the quick. But he trusted his rugged pony to lead the column. As the path rose higher, the patrol groped its way through the darkness. Every man dismounted and led his horse while holding the tail of the horse in front of him.

They came to a crossing where the river, swollen with rainwater, crashed through the narrow canyon. Tom Dick plunged into the thrashing current, with Butler clinging to his neck, and the others began to follow. After climbing the far bank, Butler told his orderly to shine his lantern on the foaming black waters to guide the men across. As the light danced on the churning river and the bobbing heads of the horses and soldiers, rifle fire suddenly broke out. Bullets flew from all directions. The Cacos—the word meant birds of

A HAITIAN GENDARME SHOWS OFF A "BLACK VENUS" TO BUTLER'S MEN.

BUTLER'S MARINES CHASED THE REBELS INTO THE MOUNTAINS, WHERE BLACK MAGIC RULED.

prey—had waited until that moment to swoop down on the marines.

Butler's savvy soldiers flattened themselves against their horses' backs as the metal whizzed through the air. The bullets tore through a dozen of the steeds, who whinnied and flailed in the water, but all the men made it safely across.

Butler led the marines up the riverbank, crawling through the mud on their hands and knees to higher ground. As his men caught their breath, Butler ordered First Sergeant Dan Daly to set up their machine gun.

"It was lost in the river, sir," Daly told him.

"Well, we'll do the best we can without it," Butler said.

But Daly, a tough Irishman from Chicago who had marched with Butler in China, took it upon himself to retrieve the machine gun. He jumped back into the water, with rebels pouring fire at him, and found the gun still strapped to a dead horse on the riverbank. Daly then coolly hoisted the gun and ammunition onto his back and clambered up the bank to the patrol.

Even with the machine gun, Butler realized they were sitting ducks. He ordered his men to keep moving forward. In the dark and rain, they could see only three or four feet in front of them. The Cacos kept pace with them in the bush. The marines were wet and shivering. But they felt a deeper chill when the Cacos began blowing on their conch shells. It was the ancient sound of slave revolts and voodoo ceremonies. The marines had heard the hair-raising tales of human sacrifice and cannibalism. The incessant blasting on the conch shells made their blood run cold. The Cacos added to the marines' torment by calling out to them in the pitch darkness and telling them in Creole how they were going to chop their bodies into pieces when they caught them.

One unfortunate marine named Sergeant Lawrence Muth had met such a fate in a different encounter. After he was captured in battle, the rebels separated Muth's head from his body and stuck it on a pole. Then,

TAKE A LOOK AT THIS!

THE ONLY WAY INTO THE REBELS' FORT WAS THROUGH A DARK DRAINAGE TUNNEL.

BUTLER HESITATED. BUT THEN HE AND TWO OF HIS MEN PLUNGED INTO THE MURKY HOLE.

AS BUTLER AND HIS MEN EMERGED FROM THE OTHER END, THEY WERE SET UPON BY A PACK OF REBELS.

according to one rebel leader, "we opened the chest and took out the heart. It was very large. And we ate of it, to partake of the courage of your Leftenant Muth. It was a glorious day."

Now—with the night full of eerie noises and their heads full of nightmares like Muth's—even Butler's most leathery veterans began praying to God to get them safely to daylight.

The marine patrol did survive the night. And just before dawn, Butler unleashed his enraged men on their tormentors. "Just go for those devils as soon as it's light," he whispered to them in the dark. "Move straight forward and shoot everyone you see."

That's what the marines did. Charging a hill where the Cacos were hunkered down, Butler and his men promptly killed 75 of the rebels and drove the rest into the bushes. Afterwards, their rage still not spent, the marines set fire to the nearby village of straw huts that had given the Cacos shelter.

The expedition was vintage Butler, full of bushwhacking ingenuity and raw courage. But the backbone of the rebel resistance was still not broken. Word soon came to marine headquarters in Cap-Haitien that the last rebel army was digging in at Fort Riviere, an old French bastion high atop a peak called Montagne Noire. The mountaintop itself—a sheer, stony pinnacle rising 4,000 feet into the clouds—seemed an impossible trek. But the fort, with its massive walls of brick and stone and 25-foot-high battlements, was even more daunting. Colonel Cole thought it was unassailable.

Once again, Butler dismissed his commander's concerns. He could take the fort with 100 handpicked men. Cole would have scoffed, as he often did, at Butler's swashbuckling ideas, but not after the leatherneck's recent mountain heroics. This time he quickly agreed to let Butler try the impossible.

The plan was to march through the night and charge the fort in the early morning. The trail was rough and badly marked. As night fell, Butler and his soldiers clawed their way up rocky ledges.

Some of Butler's patrols in Haiti's interior had been almost leisurely. He and his men would marvel at the island's beauty, the lush green ferns and pink flamingos, the abundant fruit trees—orange, lime and mango—from which they could pluck juicy treats. The island women were also a delight to behold. The soldiers would sometimes stumble upon "black Venuses" bathing naked in the mountain streams. The beauties made no effort to cover themselves. The marines' presence seemed "a matter of indifference to them," one of Butler's lieutenants reported in his journal.

But the Fort Riviere expedition was all grim business. At dawn, Butler's force reached the mountain forests just below the rebel stronghold. By now, word of the impending marine assault had spread through the area. The chilly early morning was taut with silence. Suddenly, a group of women in brightly colored bandana turbans came down the trail toward the marines. Butler immediately knew what this meant. The Cacos intended to stand and fight. The rebels always sent away their loved ones before a battle.

Butler had split up his force into three units, which approached the old fort from three different directions. At seven in the morning, Butler's company of 24 men and three officers came to the edge of the forest. The fort's massive walls loomed above them, about 100 feet away. The rocky slope in front of them had no cover, not a single bush. According to voodoo wisdom, Fort Riviere was protected by the gods, and from where Butler stood, it certainly looked that way.

Butler could not see any rebels on the walls, but he knew that as soon as the marines moved into the clearing, rifles would instantly poke through the embrasures and begin spitting lead. Butler also saw that his group would have to charge the fort by themselves. The other two companies had taken paths that became so steep they were almost perpendicular, so all they could do was provide supporting fire.

At seven-thirty, Butler blew his whistle and his company rushed up the barren slope. As he expected, the Cacos suddenly materialized on the parapets and began blazing down at them with their rifles. The mad spurt to the fort's walls, with bullets pinging all around him, exhilarated Butler. As usual, he felt pumped full of life in the heat of action.

Now he and his men were hugging the walls of the fort. They were safe from the rebels' fire here, but they quickly discovered there was no easy way to get inside since the original entrance had been closed with stones and bricks. As the marines cautiously inspected the fort's perimeter, they came upon a drainage hole in the wall. The hole was about four feet high and three feet wide, and it extended about 15 feet into the fort's interior.

Who would be the first man into the dark hole? Butler knew it had to be him. "It was I who had brought the crowd up there. It was I who had bragged how easy it would be to take the fort. So now it was up to me to lead the procession."

As Butler tried to muster his nerve, gunfire began echoing through the tunnel. The rebels realized that the marines had discovered the opening. Butler could not bring himself to plunge into the dark, bullet-riddled hole. It seemed like certain death. For once, his courage failed him. But while

BUTLER WON HIS 2ND MEDAL OF HONOR.

Butler wrestled with his fear, Sergeant Ross Iams, standing next to him, muttered, "Oh, hell, I'm going through." Iams disappeared into the hole, immediately followed by Butler's orderly, Sam Gross. That's all it took for Butler. He plunged in behind them.

As the three men crawled single-file through the tunnel, a rebel at the other end fired directly into their faces. Miraculously, the bullet whizzed past all of them. Before the rebel—a huge, muscular man stripped to the waist—could reload and fire, Iams sprang out of the tunnel and shot him. The big man spun around and sprawled in the dirt.

As Gross and Butler popped out of the tunnel and joined Iams, dozens of Cacos came charging at the three marines. One ran directly at Butler with a big club. Butler fired his automatic but missed. Just as the rebel was about to shatter Butler's skull, Gross took him down with a well-aimed bullet.

Now the rest of the company came pouring out of the tunnel. The grounds of the fort became a frenzy of bloody combat—man against man. The Cacos were brave but undisciplined fighters. In the passion of battle, they abandoned their rifles—which they were not trained to use—and resorted to primitive weapons. But swords, clubs and rocks were no match for the marines' carbines and pistols. After 15 minutes, Butler and his men prevailed, killing every rebel who didn't flee over the walls.

Afterwards, the marines searched the rebels' bodies and then hurled them into a big hole in the center of the fort. Among the dead was the rebel leader, General Josefette, a former government minister who threw himself into battle wearing a high hat and frock coat. Watching the general's body being dragged towards the hole, his brass watch chain making a trail in the dirt, Butler suddenly felt miserable. The Haitians' efforts to resist the marines—with their superior arms and training—seemed so futile and tragic. What was the point to all this?

While Butler's mood was dark after the victory on Montagne Noir, his military superiors were elated. Marine officials reported to Washington that Butler dynamited the fort after taking it: "When the last stones of the old structure were destroyed, the revolutionary hopes and ambitions of the north Haiti Cacos were buried beneath the ruins of Riviere."

The daring capture of Fort Riviere would win Butler, Iams and Gross Congressional Medals of Honor. It was the second time Butler had won the honor—making him the most decorated American soldier of his day. But his soldiers' approbation meant much more to him than any ribbons or certificates from Washington. He later shrugged off his courageous performance at Fort Riviere as a "stunt."

Butler's "stunts" soon became more spectacular—and more disastrous for Haitian independence.

PORT-AU-PRINCE, JUNE 1917

Haiti's National Assembly was in an uproar. Major Smedley Butler was storming through the doors of the legislative hall, leading squads of gendarmes from the national police force that he had organized to maintain martial rule on the island. Before Butler's armed intrusion, the legislators were on the verge of rejecting an American constitution imposed on them by the U.S. State Department—and written by a young Navy official named Franklin Roosevelt. Instead, the assembly was about to pass a constitution that would make it more difficult for U.S. banks and corporations to buy up Haiti's land and resources.

But the marine officer's dramatic entry jarred the legislative proceedings to a halt. Butler was immediately greeted by a loud chorus of hissing. The marine's loyal Haitian guard—long used to settling political disputes with bullets—cocked their rifles. They were surprised when Butler quickly ordered them to put down their weapons.

As Butler and his armed gendarmes marched to the front of the hall, he waved a decree signed by Haiti's president, Philippe Dartiguenave, dissolving the assembly.

"The assembly is shut down by order of the president!" shouted the raspy-throated Butler, as an aide repeated the order in French. "Leave the building!"

The uproar grew deafening. Furious legislators jumped to their feet, overturning chairs and knocking over tables. Again Butler had to stop his gendarmes from spraying the assembly with gunfire.

Butler handed the decree to Stenio Vincent, the distinguished, silver-haired president of the assembly. Vincent wearily put on his pince-nez glasses and began to read the document. The veteran politician

> **BUTLER, NOT DARTIGUENAVE, WAS HAITI'S TRUE RULER.**

IN OCTOBER 1921, BUTLER TESTIFIED BEFORE A SENATE COMMITTEE ON THE CONTROVERSIAL U.S. OCCUPATION OF HAITI. THE COMMITTEE HEARD TERRIBLE TALES...

...OF MARINES TORCHING VILLAGES.

SHUTTING DOWN HAITI'S NATIONAL ASSEMBLY AT GUNPOINT.

AND MAKING PRISONERS DIG THEIR OWN GRAVES.

BLAM

BLM

BLAM

knew that President Dartiguenave was an American puppet, and that he had been strong-armed by Butler into signing the decree. But there was nothing Vincent could do. The house of Haiti's people, the final remnant of the nation's century-old democracy, was about to disappear.

Vincent looked directly into Butler's face. *"Merde!"* the cultured statesman spat out. Butler felt he had been slapped. With a stricken look on his face, Vincent gaveled for order and announced that the assembly hall must be cleared. Grumbling and fuming, Haiti's legislators were then herded into the street by the gendarmes, who bolted the doors behind them.

So began the most disorienting period of Smedley Butler's long military career. He had loyally served his country in battle for two decades, even when the reasons for fighting seemed dubious. But now his government had turned him into a tropical despot. In the name of democracy, he had terminated democracy. For more than a year, Butler would in effect rule Haiti, maintaining control of the country through his well-armed, well-trained Gendarmerie—his "chocolate soldiers," as he fondly called them—and, when needed, the 1,000-strong U.S. Marine force garrisoned in Port-au-Prince and Cap-Haitien.

During his strange rule, Butler maintained a curious relationship with Philippe Dartiguenave—the rotund, genial front man whom the Americans installed in the presidential palace. It was part tragedy, part farce. Butler called him a "good-natured hippo" and an "old rogue." Dartiguenave would sometimes try to outmaneuver Butler, grabbing desperately for some real power. But he knew, in the end, that the tough marine was the only sentinel that stood between him and the outraged Haitian people.

Despite his patronizing attitude towards his political partner, Butler would have given his life for Dartiguenave. In fact, he once fought against frothing Caribbean waves to save the oversize president after they had both tumbled off a madly seesawing presidential barge into the sea.

Imperial rule proved seductive, even for the hard-bitten, no-nonsense Butler. While he presided over Haiti's affairs, he brought his family—which now included Ethel, "Snooks," Smedley, Jr., and Tom Dick—to Port-au-Prince and settled them in a palm-shaded manor on a terraced hillside, with wide verandas that overlooked the city. Their life in Haiti was the most luxurious the imperial warrior and his family had ever enjoyed. The Butlers were waited on by a staff of servants—including a former Caco rebel who kept dedicated watch over the children, once tracking down and threatening to kill a voodoo man who had tried to put a curse on Snooks by pinching her bare leg.

Butler's ambition was "to make Haiti a first-class black man's country." He wanted to leave Haiti in a more civilized state than the marines had found it. His regime did give the mountainous and wild country its first paved highway and modern sewers. But the new roads were not simply an expression of American generosity—they helped the marines control Haiti's remote and untamed areas. Butler built them by reviving the old French corvée system, with gendarmes rounding up villagers and forcing them to work on the construction.

Butler liked to think of these road crews as public works projects. He took pride in feeding the workers well and treating them humanely. They were even allowed to hold traditional voodoo ceremonies and dances at night. Marine guards would sometimes slip away from camp to spy on the naked celebrants, writhing and moaning around fires and smearing their sweaty bodies with the blood of sacrificial goats.

HUNTING HAITIANS
FOR SPORT

The dark secrets of U.S. rule in Haiti, long hidden from the American people, finally came spilling out in 1921 during a Senate inquiry. The committee, presided over by Senator Medill McCormick of Illinois, heard shocking accounts of marine violence and depravity.

One marine lieutenant, driven mad by his tour of duty in the voodoo nation, ordered a group of prisoners to dig their own graves and told two of his soldiers to shoot them and roll their bodies into the freshly dug holes. When the two privates deliberately fired wide to save the wretched Haitians—and their own souls—the officer raised his pistol and finished the job himself.

Marines strung up prisoners on beams to interrogate them and subjected them to the "water cure" and other medieval tortures. They rampaged through villages, killing fathers in front of their children and raping girls as young as eight years old.

Hundreds of unwilling people—bricklayers, fishermen, churchgoers—were kidnapped by the American-trained gendarmes and forced to work as slaves on road construction crews. The Haitians were sometimes roped together so tightly, testified an American Baptist missionary who witnessed a number of such horrible scenes, that their arms looked "like jelly or raw beef." When the slave laborers tried to escape, the gendarmes shot them down.

A marine doctor who treated a number of the victims said the rampant abuse deeply shamed him. "It is a disgrace to the United States, and to us all as American people."

The Senate inquiry was brutally revealing for its day. The hearing was the direct result of tireless lobbying

Senator Medill McCormick

by African American journalists and civil rights activists like James Weldon Johnson. A diplomat, poet and songwriter, Johnson traveled to Haiti in 1920, after being named head of the NAACP, to investigate reports of U.S. atrocities. Johnson met with the political elites in Port-au-Prince, who complained bitterly about how the marines had imported the violent racism of the American South to their once-free black nation. Then he drove into Haiti's mountainous interior, where he gathered eyewitness reports of American mayhem. Some of the worst stories came directly from marine officers, who—after being plied with rum—told Johnson that hunting down Haitians was "a great adventure and a very thrilling sport."

Smedley Butler was also called to testify, and he took a pugnacious attitude toward the proceedings. Though the worst abuses occurred after Butler left Haiti, he felt that the honor of his beloved USMC was at stake. The marines were being used as scapegoats for Washington's controversial Haiti policy.

"We are only sent to these places to perform acts—we have nothing to do with the reason for which we are sent," Butler reminded the senators.

James Weldon Johnson

And during their tours of duty on these foreign shores, marines were subject to danger and death on a daily basis. If policy makers were not going to allow marines to defend themselves, they should not send them to war.

In the end, the Senate committee gave its stamp of approval to the U.S. occupation, which would continue for another grim 13 years. (Johnson called the hearing "a whitewash.") It was Stenio Vincent—the Haitian legislative leader whom Butler forced at gunpoint to dissolve the National Assembly—who ultimately revived Haiti's democracy. After being elected president of Haiti, Vincent went to Washington in 1934, where he convinced Franklin Roosevelt to finally withdraw the marines.

But no matter what Butler called the corvée program, it was slave labor. After he finally left Haiti in March 1918, the corvée's brutal reality became shockingly clear, as less-decent marine officers took over his post and the highway was extended into the rougher, mountainous areas where no workers wanted to go.

Still, by the end of his Caribbean service, Butler could proclaim himself a friend of the "barefoot people" of Haiti. And as America's proconsul in Port-au-Prince, he even tried to establish social harmony with members of the city's Francophile high society, inviting them to parties at his house, where marine officers defied racial taboos and danced with mulatto beauties.

After years in Haiti, New York seemed like OZ.

But for Haitians, Butler would always be the symbol of a white occupation force that had crushed the island's independence.

Haiti got under Smedley Butler's skin. He did not go native, like some marines, who took up with Haitian women and abandoned their American identities. And he did not become a bloodthirsty savage, like other soldiers, who raped and murdered and robbed Haiti's powerless people. But, in a way, he became like a tribal chief: he held absolute power over an entire nation.

The strangeness of it all eventually became too much for Butler. He was no potentate, he was a fighting man. As the Great War in Europe began enfolding America, Butler lobbied Washington to send him to France. He wanted to be on the front lines of a "real war." For months the War Department resisted his entreaties; he was too good a colonial governor.

Finally, Butler persuaded his superiors to let him return to the States by arguing

he needed emergency dental work. His rotting teeth—the legacy of years of bad food and worse dental care—had finally succeeded in bringing him back to the naval hospital in Philadelphia.

Sailing into New York Harbor, Butler felt as dazed as if he were coming upon the Emerald City of Oz. Years had passed since his last visit to the United States. He felt like a visitor to his own country. The languor of the tropics was still in his blood, and the noise and bustle of Manhattan banged on his senses.

In Haiti, he was the other. But in New York too people now looked at him as if he didn't belong. Butler had returned from the tropics without an overcoat. All he had to ward off the late winter chill was a light yellow flannel uniform that had been made for his Haitian soldiers. His face—deeply bronzed from years in the Caribbean sun—seemed even darker against the buttery tone of his outfit.

As Butler made his way through the Penn Station throng, heading for the train to Philadelphia, he seemed to be the object of curiosity. Settling into the train's smoking compartment, he noticed the man across from him eyeing him intently. Finally, the man spoke up.

"What nationality are you?"

Butler, America's most decorated fighting man, just laughed.

The man could not let it rest. "Well," he demanded, "what army do you belong to anyway?"

Butler knew what the man was getting at. Should he be sharing a compartment with this exotic, dark-hued fellow?

Butler looked directly at the man. "The Haitian army," he replied.

The man turned to his companion. "I told you he wasn't a white man."

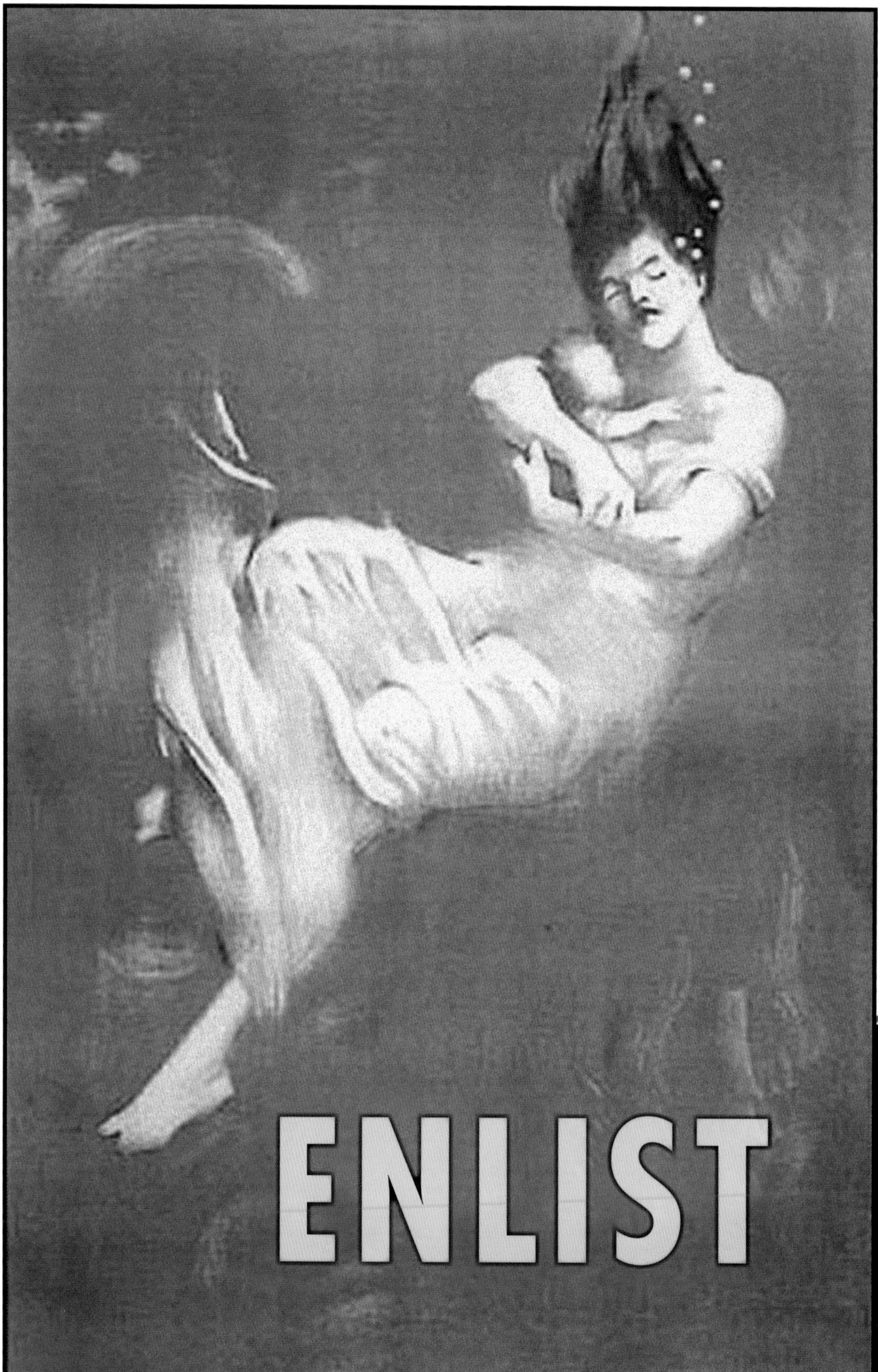
ENLIST

Act 4

Johnny, Get Your Gun

ABOARD THE USS HENDERSON, *ATLANTIC OCEAN, SEPTEMBER 1918*

They were two days out to sea when the plague hit.

Smedley Butler was finally on his way to the Great War in Europe, leading the U.S. Marines' 13th Regiment. *Thirteen*. He always thought it was his lucky number. Before the troop ship sailed from Hoboken, Butler rounded up 13 black cats as mascots and nicknamed the 13th Marines the "Hoodoo Regiment." But the black magic could not protect them.

The ship carried 4,000 soldiers stuffed into swaying hammocks below deck. Many of the doughboys, unused to the rising and plunging of the sea, were already in a miserable state. And when the first signs of Spanish influenza, the deadly scourge sweeping the world, appeared among Butler's closely confined marines, the entire vessel seemed damned.

Those stricken were wracked with violent coughs and raging fever. The unlucky ones soon grew worse—you could tell them by the blue tint of their cheeks, as their lungs filled with a bloody froth and they choked on their own fluids. Some began hemorrhaging through their noses. The sleeping quarters below became a dungeon of torment, filled with the desperate sounds of men gasping for life and the final sighs of those greeting death.

71

BUTLER SURVIVED THE ATLANTIC CROSSING, BUT HIS REGIMENT WAS FLU-RIDDEN AND MISERABLE AS IT REACHED THE SOGGY CAMP IN BREST.

Of the regiment's 4,000 men, more than 1,200 came down with the dread infection during the Atlantic crossing—and among the stricken was Butler. By the time he crawled out of his sick bed, 100 of his men were dead, including some of his favorite officers.

His ordeal was just beginning.

As the 13th Regiment sailed into harbor at Brest, on France's cold and wet Brittany coast, a gray mist shrouded the coastline. Standing on the bridge of the lighter that was to carry them ashore, Butler looked down at his pale, shivering troops. They were a pitiful sight. He could not bear to see them this way. They reminded him of his old nightmare, the one in which his comrades were rowed across the Hades while he stood helplessly on the shore of the living.

Butler called down to his men. "Do you suppose you could sing?"

Some soldiers might have thought their commander had gone mad. But these boys embraced Butler's crazy vitality like a life-saver. With a nightmarish voyage behind them, and even greater horrors awaiting them on the front, Butler's thrumming energy felt like their only hope. Like drunks in midnight choir, the entire regiment burst into the lusty strains of that old saloon ballad "Sweet Adeline." Butler sang along with them:

Sweet Adeline,
My Adeline,
At night, dear heart,
For you I pine.

In the gray stillness of the morning, the marines' thundering serenade echoed off the docks and rattled down the cobblestone streets of Brest, the medieval seaport town overlooking the harbor. The Yanks were coming.

BREST. — *Vue sur le Port de Guerre.* — L.L.

After they docked, Butler marched his men up a hill toward Camp Pontanezen, the old French military barracks once used by Napoleon's army, where the great waves of American troops washed ashore and stayed until they were sent to the Western Front. The men of Hoodoo Regiment were still singing as they climbed the hill, but when they got to the top, they suddenly stopped.

Below them was a vast sprawl of khaki-colored tents, which seemed to be sinking in a sea of ooze. The dull metal sky above made the picture all the more bleak. As the regiment made its way through the camp, they were assaulted by sour smells. There was no drainage, and the filthy runoff from the mess hall and latrines simply soaked into the mud. Butler and his men could tell from the hacking sounds in the sick stations and the listless feel of the place that the flu epidemic was sweeping through this dismal mud hole too. "Shivering cold, bleak, death-stricken—a hell of a place." That was Butler's first impression of the camp that would be his home for the next year.

Butler found out that 65,000 soldiers had been packed into a camp that was originally built for 1,500. More than 12,000 of the doughboys were suffering from influenza, and hundreds were dying each day.

The day grew bleaker still when Butler discovered that spinal meningitis had broken out among his troops. His regiment was quarantined inside a pen of mud walls. All the soldiers had to shield themselves from the wind and wet fog of the Brittany coast were the pup tents on their backs. There was no wood for fire. As they pitched camp, Butler and his men were drenched by a frigid, unrelenting downpour. Their muddy estate was soon one enormous puddle.

That evening, Butler assembled his 4,000 men. They stood, row upon row, in the rain and the squish. He told them they were going to have a songfest. His own voice was terrible; he was a croaking frog.

But he played choral leader at the top of his lungs, hopping from one song to the next with his shivering soldiers. Together, they made it through the night.

Every evening for the next two weeks, Butler repeated the ritual. He was overwhelmed by the men's heart, how they kept singing even as they slogged through their duties during the day. "I myself have never seen such men," he wrote home. "It brings a lump to my throat whenever I see them, which is all the time in fact, as my little tent is right in the middle of theirs. We all eat the same food and are determined to fight it out together."

Finally, a telegram arrived from General Pershing, commander of the American Expeditionary Force, with word of Butler's new assignment. Ripping open the envelope in his soggy tent, he could not believe his eyes. He let out a violent roar. The AEF was breaking up his regiment and sending his men to different posts all over France. And he would remain right here in the mud. He was the new commander of Camp Pontanezen!

Butler raged like a wounded animal. He blamed Marine Commandant George

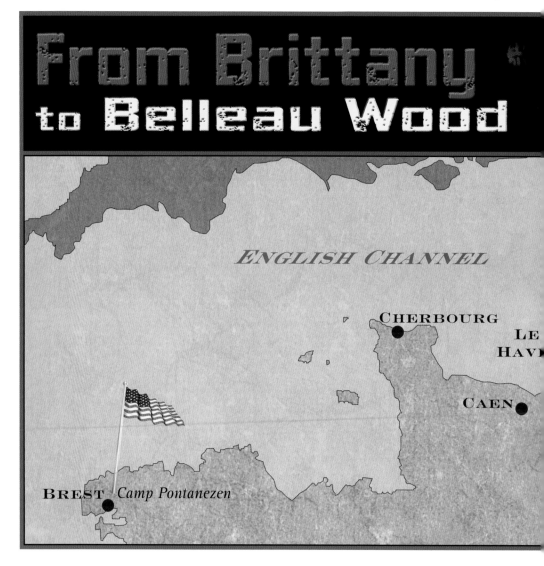

Barnett, "a weak old woman" who had never seen combat. Butler was convinced that the top brass was out to sabotage his career. "Swivel-chair commanders," he called them. And so did his father, who had long used his perch on the Naval Affairs Committee to harass these soft-bottomed generals. Now they were getting back at Butler. He would never get to see action in Europe, at least not the kind he had thrived on. He would be stuck in the cold muck of Brest.

At the time Butler took over Camp Pontanezen, it was becoming a national scandal. The first two months he was there, nearly 2,000 soldiers died of influenza. There were demands for military investigations and congressional hearings. "Our boys are dying like pigs," railed a Missouri congressman, who blamed "the criminal carelessness of the War Department."

As it turned out, the War Department—under growing public fire over the squalid camp—had given Butler the dirty job not to sink his career, but out of desperation. The generals knew Butler was a man of action, the type of leader who could get things done.

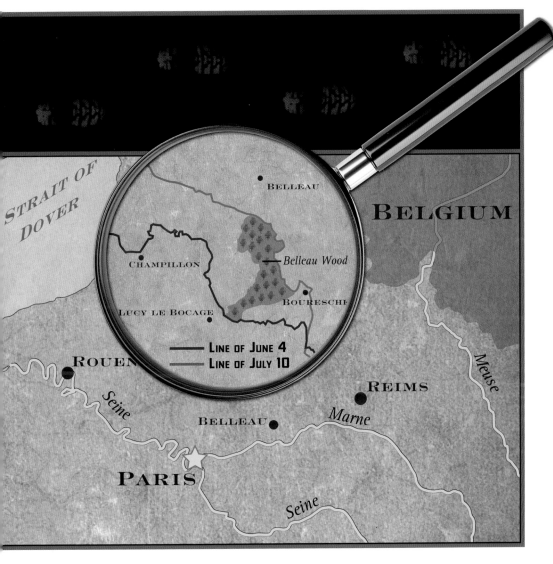

BUTLER AND HIS SOLDIERS STORMED PAST THE WAREHOUSE GUARDS TO TAKE THE DUCKBOARD. IT WAS THE ONLY WAY TO GET HIS MEN OUT OF THE CAMP'S SEA OF MUD. THE MUD WAS BUTLER'S ENEMY. THOUSANDS OF MEN WERE LYING IN IT AT CAMP PONTANEZEN, VICTIMS OF THE SPANISH INFLUENZA. THE FIRST DAY BUTLER TOOK OVER THE CAMP 250 SOLDIERS DIED. "OUR BOYS ARE DYING LIKE PIGS," A CONGRESSMAN RAILED.

B-BUT...YOU DON'T HAVE THE PAPER WORK!!

BUTLER SOON TURNED THE SWAMP INTO A MODEL CAMP. HE BUILT THOUSANDS OF WARM TENTS AND LIFTED HIS MEN'S SPIRITS BY SERENADING THEM WITH THE HELP OF HIS REGIMENTAL BAND. HE ALSO KEPT THE CAMP HAPPY WITH LOADS OF ICE CREAM-1000 GALLONS A WEEK. HE EVEN BUILT A THEATER AND BROUGHT VAUDEVILLE SINGERS AND COMEDIANS TO ENTERTAIN THE TROOPS. THE SOLDIERS LOVED HIM FOR IT. "GENERAL DUCKBOARD," THEY CALLED HIM. "I'D CROSS HELL ON A SLAT IF HE GAVE THE WORD," SAID ONE.

BUT MANY OF HIS MEN LOOKED FOR JOY WITH THE WHORES OF NEARBY BREST. THOSE WHO GOT THE CLAP WERE PLACED IN THE SEGREGATION CAMP UNTIL CURED. MILITARY INSPECTORS AND MORAL REFORMERS FUMED ABOUT THE SWARMS OF PROSTITUTES. BUT FRENCH OFFICIALS SAID THEY COULD NOT INTERFERE WITH THE LIVELIHOOD OF LOCAL CITIZENS. AND GENERALS LIKE BUTLER FOUND IT HARD TO CLAMP DOWN ON THE FLEETING PLEASURES OF MEN WHO SURVIVED THE HELL OF THE WESTERN FRONT OR WERE HEADED THERE.

After venting his fury, Butler quickly got down to work. In a letter to his parents, he vowed, "I will do all in my power to make these poor, miserable, wretched sick soldiers who pass by the thousands through here, as comfortable and happy as my poor strength will let me." Butler would live up to his word.

Two hours after taking command of the camp, Butler was told that the *Leviathan* had just arrived with 10,000 more men on board— and 4,000 of them had influenza. The camp hospital was already overflowing, and thousands more were lying sick in the mud. Butler flew into action. He released his own regiment from quarantine so they could help carry the sick on improvised stretchers from the docks to camp. Then he sweet-talked thousands of blankets and tents from his navy friends on destroyers anchored in the harbor. Butler ordered the old French rolling kitchens, rusting in the mud, repaired and spruced up. And for the next two days and nights, the men from his regiment trudged up and down the rows of sick soldiers, ladling out hot soup and distributing extra blankets. Butler also built blazing bonfires to keep the suffering doughboys warm, even though local woodcutters charged him a stiff $75 a cord.

Butler was a whirlwind of action. From early morning to late night, he rushed from one end of camp to the next, urging his Hoodoo boys to work harder, and offering comforting words to the ailing. On his first day as commander, the camp lost 250 men to the epidemic. Within weeks, the death count was negligible.

Through it all, Butler kept up the music. His regimental band, a 60-piece outfit led by an Italian American from Hartford named Felix Fernando, provided him with heroic support. Fernando's men were also suffering—they had lost two band members to influenza during the ocean crossing. But they played night and day, with little time for rest, entertaining the young soldiers stretched out in the muck—jazz, dance tunes, marching songs, love ballads. Anything the doughboys wanted to hear, anything that reminded them of home and a soft hand on their cheek.

Butler fought for his boys with all of his warrior's heart. Some days, walking down the rows of the sick, he would come upon a suffering soldier who looked so young that he reminded him of his own boys back home. "Son, where you from?" he would ask him, putting his hand on his shoulder. And he would tell Butler where home was, and what it was like, and who was waiting there for him.

He was not going to let his boys die in the mud. He was going to build a camp with roomy tents, and wooden floors, and comfortable beds. "Like a big hotel," Butler announced.

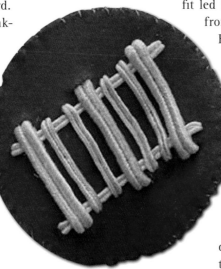

THE "DUCKBOARD" BADGE BECAME A PROUD EMBLEM FOR BUTLER'S MARINES.

But the first step was to get his soldiers out of the infernal ooze where they were spending their days. To do that he needed duckboard—the long, wood-slatted platforms that were made to be laid along the bottom of trenches. Butler decided that the duckboard would make excellent sidewalks for his sloshy camp. When he learned that the warehouses by the docks were filled with piles of the stuff, he submitted one request after the next for it, but to no avail. The old army quartermaster in charge of the warehouses feared he would be court-martialed after the war if all the duckboard could not be accounted for. Butler was informed he would have to go through proper channels.

But Smedley Butler was never the type of man to go through channels, not when

A ROUGH RIDER'S
Broken Heart

For two decades, Theodore Roosevelt had been the loudest voice of American militarism. In the country's run-up to World War I, he played the same brash role, browbeating President Wilson to go to war and questioning the scholarly president's manhood when he hesitated. He even tried bullying the administration to let him form a new volunteer division of Rough Riders so that he could be the first to 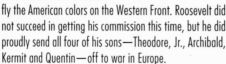 fly the American colors on the Western Front. Roosevelt did not succeed in getting his commission this time, but he did proudly send all four of his sons—Theodore, Jr., Archibald, Kermit and Quentin—off to war in Europe.

In the end, though, war would break Theodore Roosevelt's heart.

When sons Ted and Archie were both wounded on the Western Front, Roosevelt and his wife, Edith, were privately relieved, even though Archie's injuries from a shell explosion were serious enough to require multiple surgeries and a lengthy rehabilitation. The Roosevelts knew that their sons' wounds would probably save them from a worse fate.

But Quentin was not so fortunate. The youngest in the family, Quentin had been America's baby, growing up in the White House and entertaining the country with his antics.

He brought a pony into the White House to cheer up his sick brother, Archie; he convulsed reporters by calling his father "Teddy Bear" and trying to get him to perform circus tricks. Quentin was the most like his father, everyone said—adventurous, outgoing, whip-smart. He was TR's favorite, his darling boy.

Always fascinated by airplanes, Quentin dropped out of Harvard and joined the fledgling Army Air Service when war broke out. Despite his bad eyesight, he was among the first American pilots to see action. The Wilson administration had sent America's young airmen off to war scandalously unprepared and badly equipped. Quentin and his comrades flew Nieuport 28 fighter planes, French castoffs that were known for balky engines and wings that would shred during steep nosedives. Young Roosevelt's air squadron was facing the legendary Red Baron's far more experienced Flying Circus. But, like his father, Quentin was a daredevil, and he rode his old Nieuport 28 into battle like he was riding a bronco.

Quentin Roosevelt crashed to earth on Bastille Day—July 14, 1918—after a German machine gunner put two bullets in his brain. It was a newspaper reporter who came out to Sagamore Hill, the family's Long Island estate, to inform TR. "How am I going to break the news to Mrs. Roosevelt?" said the stricken father.

Roosevelt was never the same.

his men were shivering and dying. One day he decided to cut through the red tape. He rounded up 7,000 men from the camp and marched them down to the docks. Bursting into the warehouses, they brushed past the startled sentries and helped themselves to the stacks of duckboard—collecting armfuls of shovels, axes, picks and soup kettles while they were at it. Then Butler led his column, piled high with loot, back up the hill to camp. He even helped a young soldier with his load, picking up one end of a heavy slab of duckboard and hauling it through the inevitable drizzling mist.

Butler's assault on the warehouses won him the soldiers' undying devotion. After lifting them out of the muck, he was proclaimed "General Duckboard." One private

Teddy Roosevelt and his darling boy, Quentin

Mary Roberts Rinehart, a novelist who later dazzled Smedley Butler in France, was close to Roosevelt and his wife. Several weeks after Quentin's death, they invited her to lunch at Sagamore Hill. She rode out to the estate with them from the city. During the drive, the usually voluble Roosevelt sat next to his chauffeur, saying nothing. "Most of the time his head was on his breast, and I can still see his sturdy, broad-shouldered figure, stooped and tired," Rinehart recalled. "For the first time he seemed old to me, old and weary."

Rinehart sat in the rear with Edith, trying mightily to restrain her own emotions. "Mrs. Roosevelt knitted, and finally she spoke of Quentin; spoke of him sweetly, lovingly, resignedly. She believed in God, but she missed him. She missed him dreadfully. When at church she saw women with their youngest sons, their babies…

"It was too much for me, with a son in France and awful fear in my heart. To my everlasting shame I began to cry, and it was she who remained dry-eyed."

Later, at the estate, Roosevelt was very quiet and very watchful of his wife. He played with a baby, one of their grandchildren. Then he took Rinehart outside, pointing out where his children used to bury their pets. "It must have aroused old memories, old pictures," Rinehart later mused. TR abruptly turned and walked back to the house.

Even during these days of mourning, Roosevelt clung to his warrior ethos, but something darker crept into his remarks. One day he confided to a friend that it was "rather awful to know that Quentin paid with his life, and that my other sons may pay with their lives, to try to put into practice what I preached, and yet of course I would not have it otherwise." Still, he said, he wished that he could have been the one to make the ultimate sacrifice. There was nothing tragic in the death of an old man, he said—but "it is infinitely sad to have a boy die in his golden youth."

Several months later, Roosevelt died in his sleep at Sagamore Hill, after his heart failed. He was 60 years old.

summed up the entire camp's feeling: "I'd cross hell on a slat if Butler gave the word."

Some of the men entering Camp Pontanezen had already crossed hell. These were the survivors of the Western Front, who began flowing into camp a few months after Butler's arrival. While some troops were still pouring into Europe, these men were heading home.

He could tell these scarred souls right away. It broke his heart just to look at them. Felix Fernando's band music was never going to heal them. These men had stories he had never heard. They had been swept into the jaws of an industrial killing machine, the likes of which Butler had never seen. Some of them had been mangled in breathtaking ways—shorn-off noses and chins, melted faces. But the ones whose wounds were inside seemed even more deeply broken. *Shellshocked,* the doctors called it. Everything inside these men had been blown away.

What was this war? Butler found himself asking every day. *What was it doing to these American boys?*

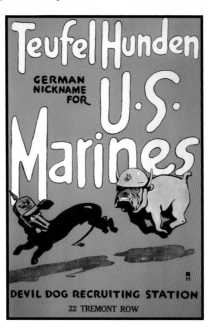

Teufel Hunden

GERMAN NICKNAME FOR U.S. Marines

DEVIL DOG RECRUITING STATION
22 TREMONT ROW

Not many of these walking ghosts wanted to talk about what they had gone through on the front. Those who did told stories of places like Belleau Wood, Soissons, Château-Thierry, Saint-Mihiel. They were stories that made life itself seem beyond human understanding.

It was the battle of Belleau Wood, in June 1918, where the ferocious image of the United States Marines was born.

Afterwards, the Germans said it was like fighting savage Indians. "Teufel Hunden," they called them—"Devil Dogs." The marines took the name proudly. But the cost of victory was dear.

The 4th Marine Brigade came rushing up the Paris-Metz highway to stop a German advance on the French capital designed to win the war before the Americans could become a factor. The German onslaught had already destroyed the British 5th Army and decimated the French forces.

As the marines hurried toward Belleau, a village set among farm fields and woods 60 miles east of Paris, they passed a shuffling, ragged line of French soldiers in retreat. With their emaciated faces and haunted stares, they reminded the Americans "more of hunted beasts than human beings," said one marine.

"Go back," the French scarecrows warned the marines. "The war is over."

The Americans—who had been told that a battle-hardened French soldier was worth several doughboys—were shocked. But they weren't about to turn back.

"Retreat? Hell, we just got here," a marine captain snarled.

The field of battle looked like a place you would choose for a summer nap. There were rippling wheat fields dotted by dewy poppies, glistening red as blood. In the distance, up a gentle slope, stood a thicket of oaks and white birch trees. Some of the American boys stopped to pick berries.

Then the idyll ended. The marines were told to dig in: Germany's best soldiers were coming, the feared Prussian Guards. They were 30 minutes away. And they outnumbered the Americans five to one.

"Dig for your lives," the officers told them. The artillery assault would come first, so they needed to burrow as deeply into Mother Earth as they could. The men dug frantically with shovels, bayonets, helmets, even spoons—whatever they had. "Digging our own graves," is how one wiseguy put it.

And then the shells began to fall. They came "with an unearthly howl, a sudden rush of air, and for one terrible moment the shell seemed to be suspended in the air as though undecided where next to blast a life," recalled one marine. Some men were driven so mad by the monstrous pounding that they wanted to jump out of their dirt holes and run into enemy fire to end it all.

One green soldier began shaking violently. He threw himself flat in the mud at the bottom of his hole, crying hysterically. The others threatened to shoot him if he didn't stop. A comrade pulled the greenie to his feet, gripped his shoulders tightly and told him he was just as scared as he was. The hands and voice acted like a sedative: the greenie kept shaking, but he quit crying.

The nights were the worst. The black sky would suddenly flash with illuminating flares, and the soldiers knew something evil was about to come. When the Germans charged, they came panting and growling into the marines' holes. The fighting was as primal as life and death. Bayonets, daggers, fists. Metal slashing through flesh and bone.

> **The Germans called the marines "DEVIL DOGS"—and the name stuck.**

The next day would be the marines' turn to attack. They crouched in their holes waiting for their sergeants to blow their whistles. Across the wheat, hidden in the woods, lay nests of German machine gunners. The American boys knew that each breath they drew might be their last.

And then came the screeching whistle.

Up and down the marine line, there was a moment of hesitation. "Suddenly we didn't want to die," was how one marine private from Texas put it.

But Sergeant Dan Daly, the bulldog-faced marine who had fought alongside Smedley Butler in Haiti, yelled out above the metallic din of the German Maxim guns.

"Come on, you sons o'-bitches! Do you want to live forever?"

And then they were out of their holes and running through the wheat, like boys in summer. There was a rush of freedom, of exhilaration after the cramped confinement of their holes. But for some boys, it ended quickly.

There was one young officer leading the charge who had tried to set an example for his men, acting older than his years. "He was the type who leads a desperate charge and cannot tell you why—he just leads. His manhood ordered it so," one of his men said.

And then, in an instant, he fell. In that instant, he became a boy again.

"Ma!" he cried out.

He screamed it loudly just once—it was the final thing that flooded into his dying heart.

"Ma-a-a!"

As the marines closed on the woods, they came upon the most outlandish sights. The dead—Americans and Germans—lay

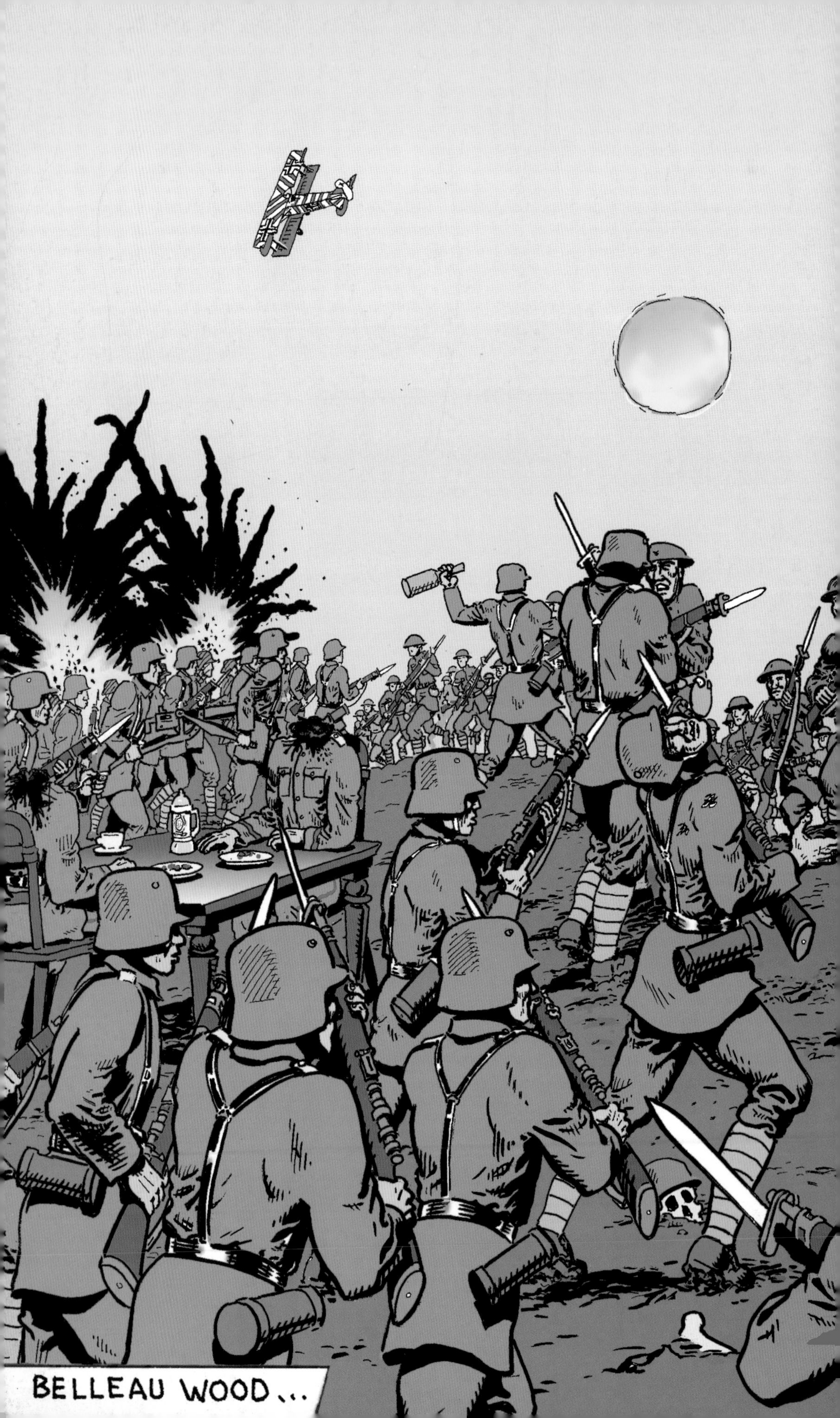
BELLEAU WOOD...

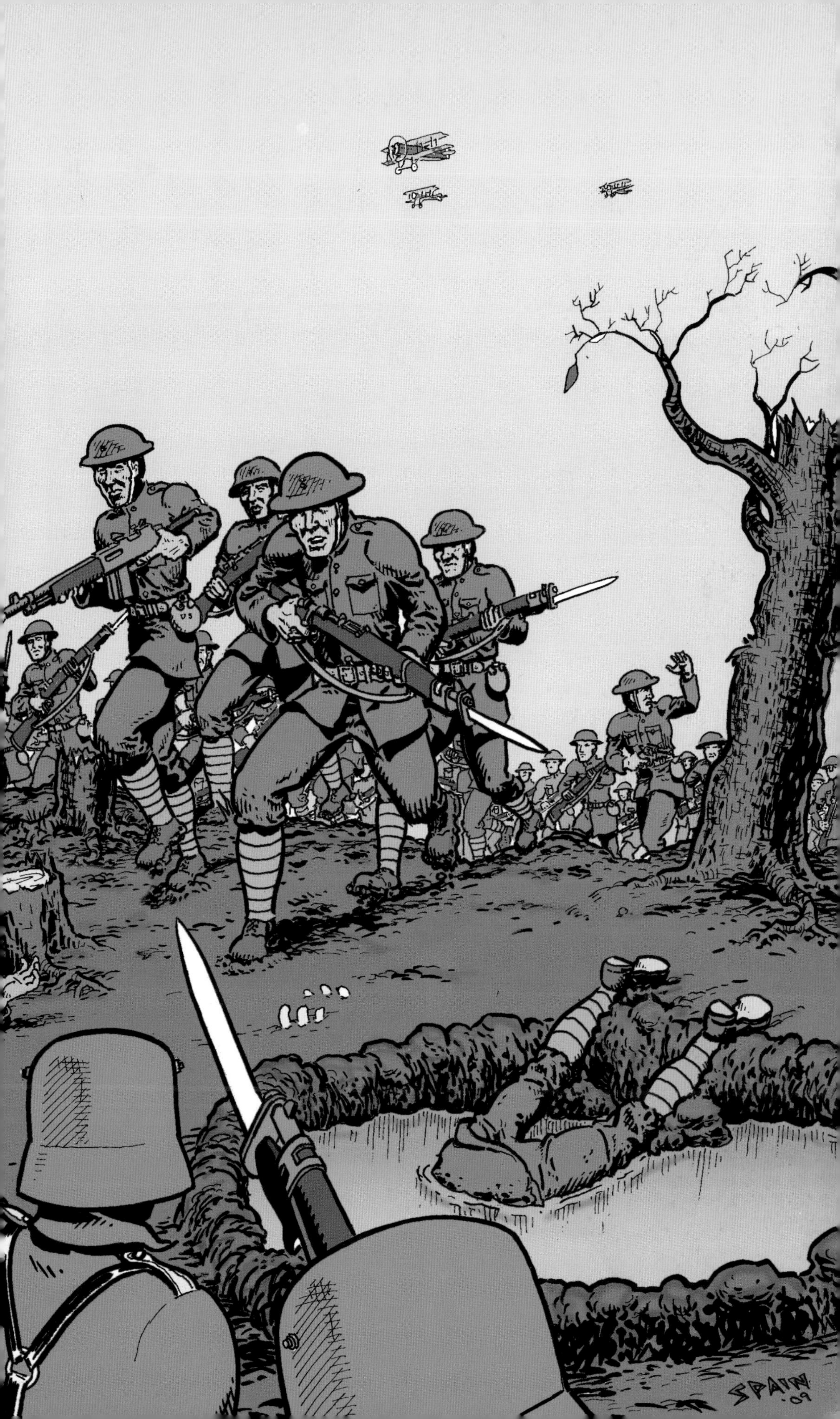
SPAIN '09

BUTLER WAS IN AWE OF WHAT THIS STRANGE WAR WAS DOING TO MEN.

promiscuously in each other's arms. One Yank still had his bayonet deep inside a Hun—both dead. A German officer sat with his knees neatly crossed at a little field table, sharing a sweet repast of cake, jam and cookies with a stocky sergeant. Both their heads were blown off. The officer still gripped his fork, as if ready to take his next bite as soon as his head could be located.

The battle of Belleau Wood went on and on, day after night. The marines charged and were pushed back, charged again and once more were repulsed. While waiting for the next mad dash into the swarms of flying metal, they huddled in their holes. The stench of rotting flesh hovered all around them. They couldn't sleep. They couldn't eat. The canned beef in their mess kits, packed in something that tasted of motor oil, turned their stomachs. "Monkey meat," they called it. It smelled like death.

Some of the shells pounding the earth around them released clouds of poison in the air. And then, up and down the line, you would hear the frantic screams.

"Gas!"

The men who still had their masks grabbed for them and desperately clamped them to their faces. The others prayed the poison would drift in another direction. When it got in a man's lungs, it made him want to claw open his chest for air. Tears streamed down his cheeks. His throat was on fire. If he lived, he would never draw a good, clean breath again.

Finally, after six sacrificial attacks, the marines took Belleau Wood, aided by a withering French bombardment. The American battalion commander sent out a simple dispatch: "Woods now U.S. Marine Corps entirely." By the time the marines overran the woods, the old hunting preserve was nothing but stumps and shards.

Nearly 2,000 Americans had died at Belleau Wood, and almost 8,000 had been wounded, many of them in hideous ways. For every man who fought there, it would always be a nightmare of the soul.

By January 1919, most of the men flowing through Camp Pontanezen were on their way home. Armistice had been declared on November 11, 1918, and the guns were silent on the front. Butler now presided over a small, bustling city. There were more than 1,100 buildings, 55 miles of plank roads, 60 miles of duckboard. Most of the camp residents now slept in tents on platforms, elevated above the muck and heated by stoves. He had expanded the hospital, which included a new psychiatric ward to treat the thousands of men whose nerves had been blown apart on the killing fields of France. There was even an ice cream plant that churned out 1,000 gallons of vanilla and chocolate a week. Traveling vaudeville acts played the camp theater—magicians, singers and bawdy comediennes like Agnes Kelly, who played an amorous widow on the prowl for her next husband. Butler loved to hear the men's raucous laughter.

He was still working himself to the bone to make the camp as clean, healthy and comfortable as possible. The doughboys coming back from the front deserved nothing less as they awaited the transport ships home.

But on New Year's Day, Butler was stunned to hear that a *Washington Post* reporter had published a scathing assessment of the camp. "Seventy thousand American soldiers are awaiting transportation home at Brest under living conditions of such wretchedness and misery that one marvels at the discipline that keeps them from breaking into open rebellion," he wrote.

"Insufficiently nourished and inadequately sheltered from the elements of a Breton winter, [the soldiers] are enduring a state of affairs that is a disgrace to the

WASHINGTON FLEW INTO A FRENZY OVER BUTLER'S CAMP.

BAKER INVESTIGATES BREST CONDITIONS

Orders Harbord to Report on Allegations of Bad Shelter and Food in Camp

CHARGES MADE BY WRITER

Says Place Is a Disgrace to the Government—Asserts Soldiers Sleep in Wet

WASHINGTON, Jan. 1—Secretary Baker today cabled to Major General Harbord, embarkation officer at Brest, directing him to make an immediate inspection of the embarkation camp there, known as Camp Pontanezen. This action followed the publication in the Washington Post this morning of a story written by George R. Brown, of its staff, who returned home Monday on the Mauretania, after four months spent on the battle fronts. He asserts that 70,000 soldiers at Camp Pontanezen live in mud swamps, while awaiting ships, and are inadequately sheltered and insufficiently nourished.

Government," the reporter continued. "I have seen mud in the front-line trenches, but I realized that I had never known what mud was until I visited this place."

Butler himself was spared the reporter's lash, which he directed primarily at Washington. But as camp commander, Butler was outraged by the newspaper's condemnation, which he felt ignored the heroic progress made by his staff in three short months. The report "hurts terribly," he wrote Ethel back home, "as we all do work so hard—in fact I get so [tired] by the time I go to bed at night that I see bright stars jumping in front of my eyes."

The War Department was well aware of how Butler's ferocious energy had lifted the camp out of its squalor. Their own inspectors had recently determined that camp conditions were "excellent" and that the men "were comfortable and well fed." But the article rekindled the controversy over Pontanezen, and military officials felt compelled to promise independent inspections of the camp.

One day a sturdily built woman in khaki pants and a heavy raincoat appeared in camp. Marching into Butler's tent, she presented him with papers that identified her as an investigator under orders from War Secretary Newton Baker. She had dark, deep-set eyes that were both penetrating and warm, a regal nose, and an auburn crown of thick, wavy locks. Butler was dazzled. But her no-nonsense manner made it clear that

BUTLER WAS AT THE MERCY OF A NOVELIST.

she wanted to get directly to work.

If he had been a book reader, Butler would have been even more impressed. The woman was Mary Roberts Rinehart, a wildly successful novelist who had revived the mystery genre in America. When war broke out, she was determined to do something useful. All four of the men in her family—including her husband, Dr. Stanley Rinehart, and her three sons—had joined the ranks, and she did not want to sit fretting about them in her Park Avenue apartment. Through her connections—General Pershing and Teddy Roosevelt were among her fans—Rinehart had finally wrestled a war assignment from Washington, inspecting battlefield hospitals and camps. And with two of her sons serving as marines in Europe, she took her job deadly seriously.

After greeting Butler, Rinehart put on thick rubber boots and set off with him on a tour of the camp. She was 42 years old, the mother of grown sons. But she plowed through the camp, matching the brisk Butler step for step. She crawled into tents, shared the doughboys' chow, and asked smart, pointed questions.

Mary Rinehart was the kind of woman who could hunt and fish, as well as engage in witty banter at a Manhattan dinner party. Her origins were humble—she met Dr. Rinehart while training as a nurse. When her husband lost the family savings in a stock market crash, she turned to crime stories, mastering the form and banging out a string of bestsellers that soon restored the family's fortune.

As Butler watched her in action, he grew more and more enchanted. Not only was she "one of the most attractive and fascinating women I've ever met, but she has brains and the understanding of a man of big caliber," he later wrote in his memoir.

Rinehart was equally impressed with Butler. She felt he was a "dynamo of energy, courage and sheer ability…a steam engine in breeches." She marveled at the way he ran the camp's myriad operations with a firm hand, but at the same time displayed a tender touch with his doughboys.

Rinehart had come to Camp Pontanezen convinced she would be filing a "blistering" report. But after three days with Butler, she wrote a glowing account from her small unheated room in a little Brest hotel. "The men were in fine condition, and cheerful," she wrote. "The food was better than in the hotel where I was stopping, in town…It was good food, hot, abundant, well seasoned." For Butler "to have produced the morale I found under existing conditions was nothing short of a miracle of ability."

Rinehart returned to the camp a month later, to make a second report, which was even more enthusiastic. Conditions "had improved incredibly," even in that brief interval, she wrote.

Years later, Mary Rinehart met Butler again, this time in Philadelphia, where he was overseeing another impossible operation, the war on bootleggers and city corruption. They would spend another three "amusing and interesting" days together.

HE AGAIN EMERGED FROM WAR A HERO.

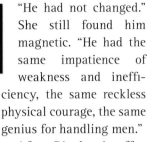

"He had not changed." She still found him magnetic. "He had the same impatience of weakness and inefficiency, the same reckless physical courage, the same genius for handling men."

After Rinehart's effusive report on the camp, Butler was visited by a parade of newspaper reporters and dignitaries, from ambitious Navy official Franklin Roosevelt to General Pershing to President Wilson. He was showered with praise. "You have brought order out of chaos," the top admiral in the navy later wrote him, "and have turned a camp, which promised to be the greatest scandal producer of the war, into what virtually amounts to a beautiful residential city."

Butler's heavily decorated chest won a string of new ribbons, including both the army's and the navy's Distinguished Service Medals, as well as the French Order of the Black Star. And he was also promoted to brigadier general—at age 37, the youngest general in marine history.

His expedition to France had begun in slop and pestilence. But by working tirelessly to take care of his men, he ended his tour of duty in glory.

In August 1919, Butler returned home, arriving in Hampton Roads, Virginia, after a much more pleasant ocean crossing than the previous year's. Before leaving to take up his new command at Quantico, the new brigadier general reassembled the surviving members of the 13th Regiment who had been scattered throughout France during the war. He talked to them about the fiery crucible they had endured. He told them of the great debt that America owed them for their service. He said he would never forget what they had done. They would be in his heart until the day he died. Marines take care of marines, he reminded them. *Semper fi.* And then he asked them to sing "Sweet Adeline" one last time.

Years later, a veteran of the 13th wrote Butler. "That talk has been remembered by more members of the regiment that I can tell you about," he told his old commander. "A good many of us never can, nor never will forget the talks that you gave us while in the mud holes of Brest, France."

Washington also pledged to take care of the returning vets. Many of them had been horribly maimed, physically and mentally, by the war. Newspapers carried stories about veterans whose postwar psyches were so eggshell-fragile that backfiring automobiles sent them screaming to hospital wards.

> Butler turned a **HELL-HOLE** into a hotel.

Some of the brave young women who volunteered as nurses were equally traumatized. One night, on board a returning troop ship, a soldier watched in helpless horror as twin sisters who had served with the Red Cross suddenly jumped over the rail, one after the other, into the freezing, dark Atlantic below.

President Wilson—who had plunged America into Europe's Armageddon to make the world "safe for democracy"—was never able to get outside the intricate architecture of his own mind and grasp the immense suffering of the young people he had sent to war. He lived in a world filled with "soap bubbles of oratory," as one senator put it. By spring 1919, it was clear that Wilson's fantasies of a new world order were being broken like butterflies against the wheel of domestic political realities and European realpolitik.

WAR DEPARTMENT
PURCHASE, STORAGE AND TRAFFIC DIVISION
OFFICE OF THE ZONE SUPPLY OFFICER,
Second and Arsenal Streets,
ST. LOUIS, MO.

Feb. 27, 1919.

From: D. S. Stanley, Colonel, Q.M. Corps, Zone Supply Officer.

To: Brigadier General Smedley D. Butler, U.S. Marine Corps , U.S.A.P.O. 716
American E.F., France.

My dear Butler:

The newspapers are so full of criticism and discussion of crimination and recrimination regarding Brest, and are so prone that I should like very much, if you have time in your very busy days to drop me a line, that you would write me as to the situation as it is now. Considering what it was in the pioneer days, and you are one of the Pioneers of Brest because conditions when you arrived there were about as bad as they could be, it seems to me that there can be little just cause for complaint by comparison with the former conditions surrounding our troops passing through that port.

With the cantonment at Pontanezen completed and with tents floored and even barracks floored, if my information is correct, with kitchen and messing arrangements completed and arranged, I should think that you would have very nearly a model camp compared with what we formerly had, and upon which, as you well remember, we received very few complaints from troops passing through. Perhaps an occasional irascible regimental or brigade commander would entertain you from time to time with a few minutes of complaints, - but as a general thing the complaints were few and far between.

As his illusions shattered, so did his health. After suffering a stroke, Wilson spent his final months in the White House drooling in his wheelchair and watching old newsreels of the war and his victory tour of Europe.

Fed up with the blood-drenched idealism of the Wilson era, the American people put simple, easygoing Republican Warren Harding in the White House in 1920. Harding promised to make war veterans a central concern of his administration. And he seemed to deliver, creating a new Veterans Bureau, with one of the largest budgets in the federal government. The new president and his energetic first lady, Florence Harding, were frequent visitors to Walter Reed Hospital. The first lady called veterans of the Great War "my boys" and ordered her chauffeur to pick them up whenever she saw them struggling down the streets of Washington on crutches.

FIRST TO FIGHT

U.S. MARINES

NOW ALL THE WAR HOOPLA SEEMED LIKE A **MACABRE JOKE**, AS THE FULL HORROR OF THE **BLOODBATH** BEGAN TO SINK IN.

But Harding soon proved to be an incompetent executive. Distracted by his frenzied sex life—which included a blackmailing mistress, illegitimate children, a broken-hearted suicide, a dead prostitute and reckless White House trysts—Harding allowed his administration to be taken over by the corrupt Ohio machine that had backed his rise to power.

In January 1923, the seamy Harding presidency began to come undone when Florence Harding—the more astute half of

the presidential couple—discovered that Charlie Forbes, the glad-handing crony she had installed as director of the Veterans Bureau, was looting the department. The man she had promised would take care of "my boys" was stealing them blind, lining his pockets with kickbacks on new veterans' hospitals and selling drugs and "medicinal" alcohol lifted from hospital cabinets.

Forbes—a dapper, chubby-cheeked, fleshy-lipped man, who plastered his red hair close to the scalp and wore round,

WAR OF WORDS

Johnny, get your gun. The war cry was popularized by Broadway entertainer George M. Cohan in his 1917 hit song, "Over There." Thousands of young doughboys marched to war in France singing the jaunty, hypnotic tune, which began, "Johnny get your gun, get your gun, get your gun/Take it on the run, on the run, run." The song's chorus swelled with a triumphant swagger that matched the mood of the country in the early months of the war: "Over there, over there...Send the word, send the word to beware/We'll be over, we're coming over/And we won't come back till it's over, over there!"

Antiwar novelist Dalton Trumbo

But years later, after America had absorbed the full horror of World War I, the rallying cry inspired a very different work, Dalton Trumbo's 1939 antiwar novel, *Johnny Got His Gun*. Trumbo was a successful screenwriter who was later blacklisted and jailed for bravely defying the government's Cold War inquisition in Hollywood. He was inspired to write *Johnny Got His Gun* after reading about a young Canadian soldier who was given a medal by the Prince of Wales after being grotesquely maimed in the Great War. In the novel, a young American serving on the Western Front wakes in a hospital, where he slowly realizes that virtually all of his body and senses have been blown away or amputated. "He was a dead man with a mind that could still think."

Red-white-and-blue pied pipers like Cohan had merrily urged "every son of Liberty [to] hurry right away, no delay, go today." By fighting the Germans, they would "make [their] Daddy glad to have had such a lad."

But the hero of Trumbo's novel has learned there is no glory in war. The soldier's body has been annihilated, but his mind can still piece together with brutal clarity exactly what his country's leaders have taken from him. His mind screams silently, trying to warn the next generation of American youth what the war makers have planned for them.

Don't let them kid you any more. Pay no attention when they tap you on the shoulder and say come along we've got to fight for liberty or whatever their word is there's always a word...

Your Song—My Song—Our Boys' Song
OVER THERE

WORDS AND MUSIC BY
GEORGE M. COHAN

If they talk about dying for principles that are bigger than life you say mister you're a liar. Nothing is bigger than life. There's nothing noble in death. What's noble about lying in the ground and rotting? What's noble about never seeing the sunshine again? What's noble about having your legs and arms blown off? What's noble about being an idiot? What's noble about being blind and deaf and dumb? What's noble about being dead? Because when you're dead mister it's all over. It's the end...You're dead mister and you died for nothing.

You're dead mister.

Dead.

Harold Lloyd eyeglasses—kept some of the booze for his own wild, Prohibition-flaunting parties. A Senate committee heard eye-popping testimony of debauchery and drunkenness at bacchanals thrown by Forbes in swank New York hotel suites and California estates, where the liquor flowed and half-naked "actresses" cavorted with the veteran affairs administrator and his guests.

When Harding finally found out about Forbes's violation of the public trust, he summoned him to the White House's Red Room and throttled him by the neck, screaming, "You yellow rat! You double-crossing bastard!"

But by then, the entire Harding administration was sinking in a sea of corruption. Meanwhile, the newspapers carried stories of destitute veterans struggling for their disability benefits. Suffering doughboys, whose every ragged breath was a reminder of gas attacks on the Western Front, fought year after year to convince the government that their ruined lungs were a legacy of the war. One-legged men, whose stumps flared like fire every time they rubbed against the heavy iron braces of their artificial legs, hobbled into Veterans Bureau offices for financial help: just something to live on until some employer would give them a chance. They waited day after day in government offices, shuffling from one desk to the next. Fill out another form, they were told, and another.

Butler made a point of visiting veterans' hospitals to see how the broken soldiers were doing, even though it was not part of his official duty. He called the hospitals graveyards of "the living dead." In Marion, Indiana, Butler came upon one where hundreds of shell-shocked veterans were kept like rabid dogs in "pens"—old barracks secured tightly with steel bars and razor wire. These boys were once "the pick of the nation"—each one had been a proud mother's son, a sweetheart's lover. And now they were mentally destroyed. "These boys don't even look like human beings," he thought.

"THESE BOYS DON'T EVEN LOOK LIKE HUMAN BEINGS."

The country had forgotten all about these ruined boys. America seemed awash in new money—billions of it made off the war. The banks got rich, the war manufacturers got rich. Government crooks like Charlie Forbes got rich. But the soldiers who fought the war were still paying for it. "War is a racket." Those were the bitter words that came to Butler as he looked around at what America was becoming.

By now he was thoroughly sick of war and the men who profited from it. After fighting all over the world for his country, Butler was finally coming home. And he was bringing the war home with him.

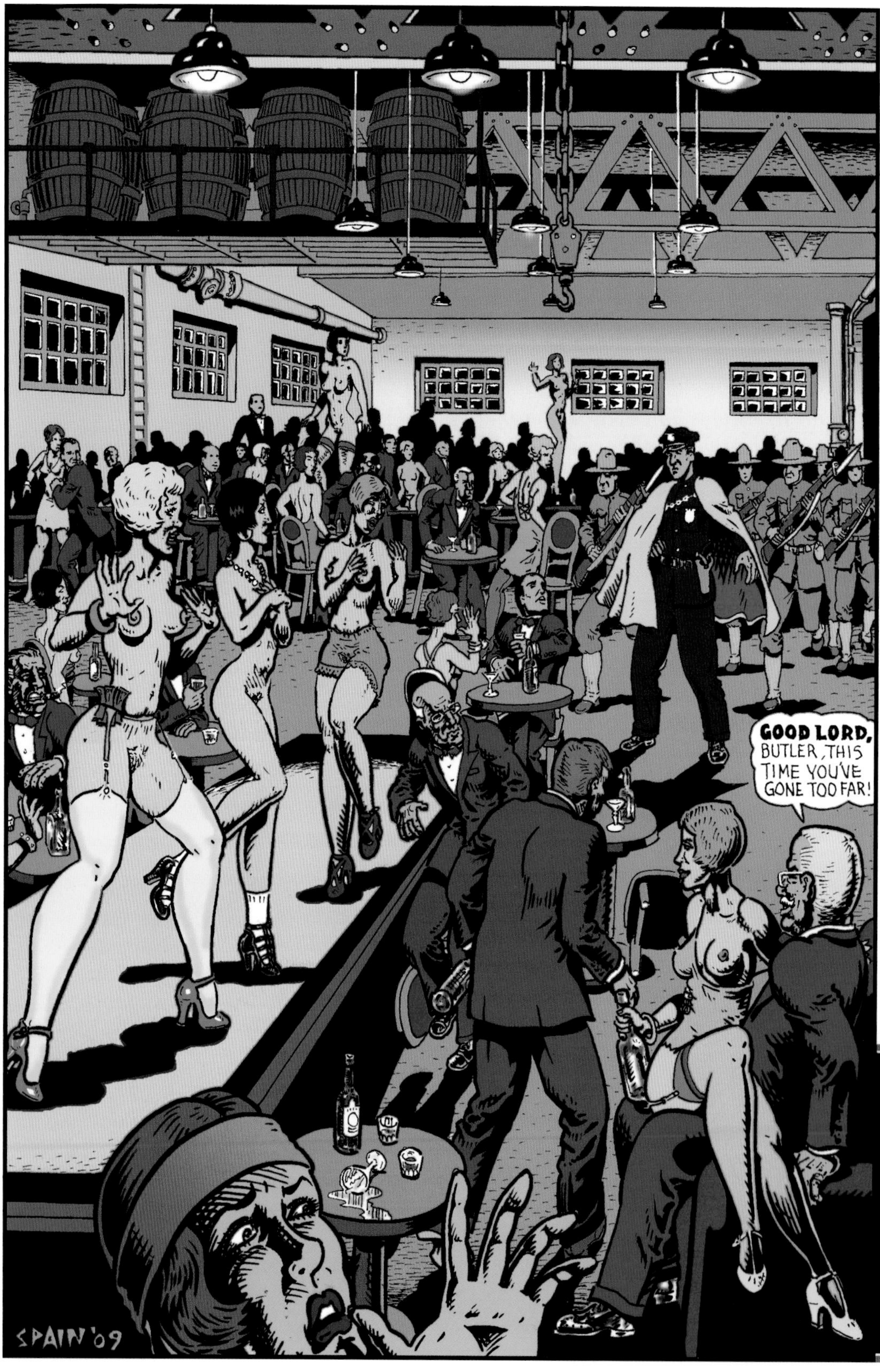
GOOD LORD, BUTLER, THIS TIME YOU'VE GONE TOO FAR!
SPAIN '09

Act 5

Badge of

Honor

Smedley Butler was riding down Broad Street in his official car when his chauffeur spotted the gangster. He was a dapper-looking fellow, and he stood on the street as if he owned it. In fact, his type did own much of Philadelphia.

Prohibition had sparked an explosion of organized crime and corruption in America. The booming traffic in bootleg booze created a new class of powerful criminals in many cities, including Philadelphia, where underworld barons spread their influence far and wide, from the local wards and precinct stations to the downtown banks.

The people of Philadelphia, feeling increasingly besieged, had just elected a mayor named W. Freeland Kendrick who promised to clean their city of its rampant vice. Kendrick, in turn, had turned in desperation to a military man to lead the war on crime—native son Smedley Darlington Butler. At first, Butler turned down the job. He bluntly told Kendrick that no one could clean up the city as long as it was run by crooked political bosses. But the mayor assured Butler there would be no political interference in his police work. He appealed to the general's sense of civic duty. The fight to preserve America's values was being lost at home, the mayor told him—right here in the city of his birth,

> **Butler's raid was said to embarrass some of the city's biggest names.**

where bootleggers, dope peddlers, stickup artists and trigger men were overrunning the cradle of American democracy.

So Butler requested a leave of absence from the Marine Corps and took the job as Philadelphia's director of public safety. It would prove to be the toughest job of his life. "Cleaning up Philadelphia," he would say, was "worse than Chinese torture or any war," because "the enemies were hidden."

Butler was not the type of man to stay behind his desk. As soon as he moved into his big, square office in City Hall, he began prowling the streets, looking for trouble. When his chauffeur pointed out the flashy dresser on Broad Street, telling Butler he was one of the most notorious gunmen in Philly, the general ordered him to stop the car.

As his limousine screeched to a halt, Butler leaped out and marched briskly toward the gangster. The gunsel's jaw dropped open—he had never been confronted by a lawman like this before. The crime-buster was wearing a uniform that he had designed himself, and inch for inch, it was as snappy as the gangster's own getup, including a pale blue blouse, gold insignia and a dashing cape with red lining. Butler's eyes were bloodshot and deeply shadowed from sleep deprivation,

after he'd kicked off his reign as public safety director with round-the-clock raids on speakeasies and moonshine stills. He looked like a man who was not to be trifled with.

Butler stuck his sharp beak in the other man's mug. "They tell me you're a bad actor." The gangster began to mumble a reply. Butler cut him off.

"Well, see this?" He pointed at a gold service stripe on his uniform. "I got this for killing your kind. Now get out of this town quick. Hear? Get out, and don't come back. Or I'll get you myself."

The Philadelphia newspapers called Butler "Devil Dog." The former marine was prepared to chase the city's gangsters to the gates of hell. Butler's first weeks in office were a frenzy of action. He shut down over 1,000 saloons, including one directly across from City Hall. He made midnight calls on police stations and, appalled by the "fat and lazy" cops he found on duty, ordered them to join the war on crime or get out. He told his men to "shoot to kill" to break the grip of the violent crime lords. You can't reason with "a mad dog," he declared. "When he's on the rampage, we can't read him homilies." He trusted only a minority of the police force to do its job, so he armed firemen with .45 caliber army revolvers and called on them to serve as auxiliary cops.

PHILLY'S CRIME WAR WAS AS WILD AS A HOLLYWOOD MOVIE.

"EVERY COP HAS A STILL IN HIS HOUSE!"
SHE SCREAMED AS THE POLICE CUFFED HER HUSBAND.

When political bosses stomped into Butler's office to demand the release of bootleggers or to try to install cronies in the police department, Butler stunned them by telling them where to go. When a gambling czar offered him $100,000 to look the other way on his bookmaking operation, Butler spilled the bribe to the press.

But his whirlwind of policing barely made a dent in the carnival of crime that was Philadelphia. Every day the newspapers carried hair-raising stories of criminal mayhem and human depravity, much of it produced by the black market in booze and its corrosive effects on municipal authority. To Butler,

who had been overseas for most of his life, it seemed as if his hometown had gone mad. The upright burg of Quaker decency where he had been raised was in danger of becoming a sulfurous, Bosch-like nightmare.

The newspapers screamed of flapper bandits and high school bootleggers, ministers falling victim to demon rum, and more depravities:

"Hooch-Crazed Man Murders His Wife and Tries Suicide."

"Gang Leader Shot After Leading 50 Men on Rampage."

"Young Woman in Hotel Opens Fire upon Crowd."

"Fusillade in Street Terminates Pursuit of Liquor Convoy."

"Rum Orgy of Boys and Girls Halted After Calls from Neighbors Swamp Police."

Shoot-outs between cops and gangsters blazed through downtown streets. Victims of bad bathtub hooch filled hospitals. Bodies were dumped in a city bog that became known as "Bandits' Cemetery."

Two ragged, unwashed girls–distraught because their mother had not stopped drinking whiskey since their father died days before–walked to the federal building and turned her in to Prohibition agents.

Detectives crashed a wedding ceremony to nab a dope ring suspect, and were forced to hold off irate guests with their pistols.

A man dying from poison liquor exhaled the name of his bootlegger, and when cops raided his joint, they found the culprit enjoying a glass of wine with a fellow policeman. Police raided a still in a house next door to a judge's residence. As they dragged off the bootlegger, his wife screamed, "Every cop in Philadelphia has

BUTLER'S CRACKDOWN BEGAN WITH CORNER SPEAKEASIES, BUT MOVED ON TO THE BIG BOYS.

BUTLER PADLOCK ON 973 SALOONS BY FIRST DRIVE

Director Announces Ninety Per Cent. of City's Vice Resorts Closed as Result of Police Raids

Ninety per cent. of the sa bling houses, and vice dens phia have closed down tight the recent police drive, Ge ley D. Butler announced ternoon.

'GET BOOTLEG KINGS,' BUTLER THUNDERS

Director Sends Jolt Through Officers Who Must "Deliver Goods or Quit"

Alcohol Flood and Reign of Bandits Stir Ire of the "Devil Dog"

BUTLER DENOUNCES FEEDING WINE TO GIRLS

He Announces Campaign to Stop It in Connection With Ritz-Carlton Padlock Suit.

PHILADELPHIA, Dec. 5.—General Smedley D. Butler, Philadelphia's Director of Public Safety, says that "feeding young girls wine and punch in fashionable hotels" has got to stop.

He made this declaration in announcing that suit would be started next week to padlock the Ritz-Carlton Hotel for alleged violation of the prohibition laws.

General Butler again served notice on his police lieutenants yesterday to clean up their districts, become more effective in the suppression of banditry, and round up more big bootleggers and bandits instead of street corner loungers, or resign themselves to demotion.

Just before the general issued, in language punctuated by spasmodic outbursts of profanity, this ultimatum to his subordinates, Federal prohibition officials here admitted the truth of the director's char

FASHIONS FOR BOBBED-HAIRED BANDITS

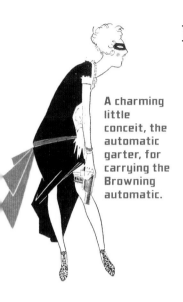

A charming little conceit, the automatic garter, for carrying the Browning automatic.

A little striped tailleur for prison wear.

The get-away gown. It allows freedom of move-ment. The little black bag is carried with this outfit.

a still in his house!" The city seemed so lawless that the Ku Klux Klan threatened to march in and restore order.

Butler was determined to take back Philadelphia from the gunslingers. But as he pushed his cops to join the war on crime, there were inevitable casualties. He was still seeing young men in uniform bleed and die, while rich men sat back and reaped the rewards.

They called her "The Bobbed-Hair Bandit." She was the second teenage flapper that year to make the wrong kind of headlines in Philadelphia. Her name was Dorothy May Rodgers, and she was just 16, but the newspapers said she was built like a full-grown woman. She was a busty 5-foot-3, and her piercing gray eyes also got your attention. Her dark chestnut hair was bobbed and combed back in the latest fashion. And when the cops caught her, she was dressed for a night on the town, in a blue silk dress, dark blue coat with fur collar, black silk stockings and black satin slippers. She was the kind of girl who could make a man do crazy things. And during their brief romance, William Paul Worth did about as many as a man could do.

They met at a party, and it was love, or something like it, at first sight. Paul Worth was a 23-year-old assistant movie projectionist. Later, a cop who knew him said Paul was always talking about the movies; the "reels of sensation" that the young man unspooled every night worked some kind of spell on the kid, the cop speculated to the press.

One evening, about a month after the young couple met, Dorothy told her mother she was going to the movies. She met Paul on the street and he took her to the theater. He never took her home. After the show,

AFTER FAILING TO HIJACK A CAR, THE KID JUMPED ON A PASSING DELIVERY TRUCK, ABANDONING HIS "SWEETIE".

MEANWHILE, THE BOBBED-HAIR BANDIT FOUGHT LIKE A HELLCAT TO FREE HERSELF.

the two checked into a hotel, registering as "Mr. and Mrs. Worth." Paul told the clerk that their luggage would be arriving the next day, but it never did.

Paul and Dorothy stayed in bed until 1 p.m. the next afternoon. They were frantic for each other; they wore each other out. Afterwards, they showered and put on their clothes. Paul was a sharp looker too, 5-foot-10, slim build, dark hair, deep brown eyes. He wore a light suit, a soft brown hat and a tweed overcoat.

> ### As the cop lay
> # DYING,
> ### Butler broke down in tears.

It was like they were living a dream and they didn't want it to end. Paul said there was a movie playing around the corner that he wanted to see, so they went. They were as young and beautiful as movie stars. But they were broke.

When they came out of the theater, it was still daylight. Something came over Paul. The spell was starting to break. If Dorothy was going to be his leading lady, he needed more money. That's when it all began.

The young lovers jumped into a taxi, and Paul told the cabbie to stop on North Tenth Street and to wait for them. He gave Dorothy a silk handkerchief and told her to put it on her face. Then they went into a grocery store and Paul pulled out a gun and stuck up the man behind the register. All the grocer had was five bucks, but as they sprinted out the door for the waiting cab, they felt rich and free.

The next day it all came crashing down. Waking up, the young couple left their hotel and walked down the street to a shoe store. Paul pointed his gun at the shoemaker's face and said, "Come across." The shoemaker tried to reason with him. "I'll shoot you," Paul threatened. But when the shoemaker started

shouting, Paul and Dorothy dashed into the street.

Everything was moving so fast, faster than a movie. Paul yelled for a passing coupe to stop, and when it did, they jumped in and Paul stuck his gat in the driver's gut. "Go like hell," he told him. The man refused. Suddenly there was a cop with his pistol drawn standing in front of the car. He called to Paul to drop his gun.

"Like hell I will," Paul shouted, jumping out of the car. The cop fired first, but Paul got off a better shot, and the bluecoat crumpled in the street. Then the young outlaw jumped on the running board of a passing butcher's delivery truck and barked, "Drive fast or I'll plug you."

Back in the coupe, Dorothy wrestled frantically with the driver, but could not free herself. "She fought like a hellcat, she bit and scratched and kicked," the driver said. It took a full five minutes to subdue her.

After the bluecoats arrested the bobbed-hair bandit, they took her to the hospital where the young cop Paul had shot lay dying, a bullet lodged in his lung. The police wanted him to identify the girl before he slipped into darkness. The officer's name was Stephen Fabeck, and he and his wife, Ruth, had a one-year-old daughter. Fabeck had survived the Great War in France, only to be cut down in the dirty war on his city's streets.

When the doctors told Dorothy there was no hope for Fabeck, she finally broke down. "I'm sorry I did it," she cried at the cop's bedside. "But I couldn't help it. He made me do it. Oh, mother, why didn't I listen?"

Dorothy's mother collapsed when informed that her daughter was the bobbed-hair bandit. She couldn't make any sense of it. "She was always an industrious girl." Even Dorothy seemed confused by her life. Later, in her cell, she was still puzzling over what she had done. "I don't know why I did it. I guess I liked him. He was my sweetie. He wanted company, and I went along. I didn't go to rob. But he had me hypnotized."

General Butler arrived in Officer Fabeck's hospital room shortly before he drifted into unconsciousness. As the general entered, the young cop tried to salute him but he couldn't. "I'm sorry I didn't get him, director, before he got me," Fabeck murmured. Butler patted him on the shoulder. "We're proud of you, Fabeck, mighty proud." Then the crusty soldier walked out of the room, closed the door and broke into tears.

There was a fury burning inside Butler over what Philadelphia—and America—was becoming, and it burst into full flame the day after he visited the dying Fabeck. America had lost its soul. It was all about guns and money. The bootleg rackets had corrupted everyone, from corner grocers with backyard stills to civic leaders whose

bank accounts were full of dirty cash. Butler was fed up. If he was going to restore law and order, he had to crack down on the big boys, not just the neighborhood speakeasies where working stiffs grabbed a beer. The downtown bankers and power brokers were the ones making the big

HIGH OFFICIALS NAMED IN HOTEL BOOTLEG LISTS

HE KNEW THE WHOLE CITY WAS CAUGHT IN A WEB OF CORRUPTION.

Capture of Man With Special Auto Holding 85 Gallons of Rum A Yields Note-book

Spectacular Raid on "101 Ranch" Climax of One Wettest Weeks in Butle Regime

Capture of an alleged bootlegger," whose list of ers is said to include name State, city and Federal offi a spectacular raid on a hou as "The 101 Ranch," mark max yesterday of one of tl weeks since General Butle Director of Public Safety ed his drive against liquor

As a fitting end to a wee 652 men were arrested enness, the police of all o ported a total of 174 arr charge over the week-e rum played a large part i sending twenty-four me tals for treatment.

Police say that the so- bootlegger" is one of t portant liquor capture in this city. The man

POLICEMAN CAUGHT IN LIQUOR RAID ON TIP OF DYING MAN

Officer Suspended When Found With Coat Off Drinking Wine

School Children Hoot Agents and Then Throw Snowballs at Patrolman

Revelations by a man dying of poison liquor led yesterday in a spectacular raid on a house in Paschall avenue near Seventy-second street, and the discovery of a policeman, his uniform coat thrown aside, sitting at a table with a glass of wine before him.

The owner of the house later was identified by the victim as the person who sold him the liquor.

William J. O'Brien, 30 years old, of Darby, is the man who was taken into the Misericordia Hospital last Saturday at the verge of death. When O'Brien's condi...

money. They were profiting from the chaos on the streets while cops like Fabeck paid with their lives. It was the same old story. Butler had seen it all his life.

After returning from the hospital that afternoon, Butler demanded to see his top lieutenants in his office. As soon as they filed in, he lit into them. He wanted them to start going after the big crooks, not just the small operators. "The jig's up," he shouted in his hoarse rasp. "From now on, you've got to start punching at everybody—or get out.

"I want bootleggers who can write checks for hundreds of thousands—not the small fry and the scum that infest the streets."

Then his voice grew quiet. "There's a boy dying in one of the uptown hospitals because a bandit shot him before he had a chance to shoot back. He didn't say 'I don't want to die.' He just told me he was sorry that he hadn't been able to get the man that got him. So they can say what they want to about a policeman, but nobody can say we're cowards."

Don't disgrace your badges, Butler told his men. Don't let fat-wallet lawyers and political bosses buy your honor. There are some things in life that should not be for sale.

EVENING, MARCH 4, 1924

Society girls in ballet costumes and even more scanty outfits pirouetted in the street. Their young escorts—dressed as Spanish toreadors, Knights of the Round-table and pirates in leather and lace—stumbled raucously after them. A crowd of less-exalted Philadelphians gathered to gawk at the spectacle. It was the Bal Masque, the annual costume ball that marked the end of Philadelphia society's winter season.

Public Safety Director Smedley Butler had announced that the police would be closely watching this year's pre-Lent fling, which attracted hundreds of the city's most diamond-studded names. There would even be undercover cops in costume mingling with the guests at the swank Bellevue-Stratford, warned Butler. And if they witnessed brazen abuse of the antiliquor laws, he would not hesitate to raid the premises and drag away the offending gents and debutantes.

> **THE TIPSY SWELLS AT THE BAL MASQUE MOCKED BUTLER'S COPS.**

Smedley Butler was tired of Prohibition's unequal enforcement. He was putting Philadelphia society on notice. From now on, the champagne-swilling rich would be subject to the same treatment as the beer-guzzling poor.

"There's no secret that I expect patrons of the Bal Masque to try to drink liquor

MAGAZINES LIKE **VANITY FAIR** TOOK
A BEMUSED VIEW OF HIGH SOCIETY **HIGH JINKS—**
BUT NOT **B**UTLER.

from hip-pocket flasks and other personal methods of supply," Butler announced on the eve of the ball. "It is the so-called 'big people' who have thus far been the most flagrant violators of the law, and I'm going to try to get them. The citizen of average means gets arrested and the courts fix drastic penalties, while the big fellows hire $100,000-a-year lawyers and worm their way out. If conditions warrant it, I'll raid the Bal Masque and in that way convince the little fellow in Philadelphia that I'm playing no favorites."

The bluebloods were outraged. Joseph Parker Norris, the chairman of the ball, urged Butler to at least pick detectives with "social graces" to monitor the exclusive event. But the general refused to coddle the Bal Masque crowd. The cops he sent that night were "just plain bulls," sniffed Norris.

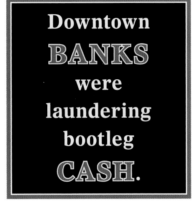

Downtown BANKS were laundering bootleg CASH.

The Social Register swells were used to getting their way, however, and they succeeded in evading Butler's clampdown that night. As the general's thick-necked undercover detectives—stuffed into ruffled shirts and sequined slippers—shouldered their way through the crowd in the Bellevue-Stratford ballroom, they noticed many of the revelers coming and going from the Ritz-Carlton Hotel across the street. At the Ritz, in suites booked for the occasion, the masked celebrants freely imbibed martinis and whiskey highballs, before staggering giddily back to the heavily policed Bellevue.

Early in the evening, the under-dressed debutantes threw on cloaks and overcoats before plunging into the street and making their way to the Ritz. But as the game wore on, Philadelphia's princesses openly mocked Butler's men, running outside dressed only in their flimsy costumes and drawing gasps from the gathering crowd. Throughout the night, Broad Street was filled with the city's finest young ladies—made up like Hawaiian hula dancers, gypsies and harem girls, and giggling and floating on a cloud of champagne bubbles.

Butler was humiliated by the high-class high jinks. The next morning, the *Philadelphia Inquirer* blared, "Bal Masque Gay Despite Presence of Police Guard: Butler's Men Are Bewildered by Constant Shifting of Merrymakers Between Dance Floor and the Ritz-Carlton Hotel Across the Street."

But Smedley Butler was not the type to accept defeat. He soon declared war on the city's wealthy scofflaws. "Get the big fellows," Butler demanded in a meeting with his top aides. "The bigger they are, the better I like it."

Weeks after the Bal Masque, the public safety director dropped a bombshell, charging that many of the city's bankers were in cahoots with bootleggers. This unholy alliance was long rumored, but the general was the first to make it a public issue.

Butler stunned the city's business community by arresting a prominent banker on dry-law violations. When two directors of another bank paid a visit to Butler to pressure him to release the executive, the general stood his ground. Later, he shot a verbal cannon across the two bankers' bow, telling the press that both of these men also profited from bootleg deposits.

Around the same time, Butler's men pulled over a suspected bootlegger who was driving a custom-built touring car. When a detective lifted the front seat of the car, he discovered a panel of five buttons, each of which opened a secret compartment containing high-grade bottles of whiskey. As he was booked at Central Station, the elegantly dressed young bootlegger maintained his calm composure, blithely informing the police that "there are men higher up back of me." In his breast pocket, the cops found a notebook containing the names of his elite clients, including a constellation of city, state and federal officials.

Butler became so aggressive in targeting the city's elite that rumors spread he was recruiting marines to raid the private orgies of the posh. According to one wild story, a squad of leathernecks with bristling bayonets—and Butler in command—crashed through the door of a bootleg warehouse, where an inebriated group of city fathers was being entertained by naked chorus girls.

Butler took aim at his biggest target when he exposed the legal distribution of "industrial" alcohol in Philadelphia, which he charged was a cover for bootlegging. More than 400,000 gallons of this alcohol were being distributed to Philadelphia manufacturers each month, all under federal permits. One of the biggest crooks in the legal alcohol racket,

Butler alleged, was a local Republican Party boss named Henry Trainer who had operated a big distilling firm in the days before Prohibition. According to Butler, the well-connected Trainer was still in the liquor business.

By taking on Trainer, Butler was challenging the city's Republican machine, which was under the control of powerful Congressman William S. Vare. But the general was also biting the hand that had appointed him—that of Republican Mayor W. Freeland Kendrick.

Kendrick had hired Butler with great fanfare as the shining symbol of his municipal cleanup campaign. But as Butler's drive went beyond corner speakeasies and started shaking up the city's establishment, Kendrick himself became increasingly rattled. In the early months of his tenure, Butler had been heaped with praise by the mayor as a heroic example to the rest of the nation. But as Butler began making clear he was not simply a hood ornament, but a genuine agent of reform, the mayor quickly began backing away from him.

"I was hired as a smoke screen," Butler bitterly realized. "The politicians were buying the reputation I had earned in 26 years' service as a Marine. I was to make a loud noise, put on a brass hat, stage parades, chase the bandits off the streets—and let rum and vice run their hidden course." Butler was not going to play their crooked

THE MAYOR TOLD BUTLER (RIGHT) TO RAID ONLY **BASEMENT BOOTLEGGERS.**

game. If he was going down, he was going with guns blazing.

EVENING, SEPTEMBER 29, 1924

Braving a rainstorm, the crowd converged on the Academy of Music, Philadelphia's grand old opera house, buzzing with civic fervor. Inside the ornate building, under the massive gilded dome with the shimmering chandelier, the seats were quickly filling up. Every red velvet chair, from the orchestra pit to the highest tiered balcony, was soon taken and the overflow was directed to folding chairs onstage and in the wings.

For the past two months, Mayor Kendrick—under stiff pressure from the Vare machine—had been maneuvering to fire Smedley Butler as the city's top crimefighter. The scrappy Butler fought back, taking his battle to the people of Philadelphia. He went on radio, appealing to law-abiding citizens to join him in his struggle with crime lords and their powerful allies in the city's establishment. He worked the press, winning over reporters with his blunt speech and theatrical heroics. He spoke in public, before women's groups, civic associations and church organizations. If you want your city back, Butler told the people of Philadelphia, you have to get off your rear ends. March, vote, tip off the cops when you see crimes in your neighborhood. A city is only as clean as the citizens demand it to be, the general gruffly told them.

Now, as Butler fought for his post, the public was flocking to his cause. The overflow crowd at the Academy of Music was filled with ministers, civic reformers, well-bred ladies—do-gooder types not usually

Civic crusaders RALLIED around him at the opera house.

given to boisterous protest. But that night, they were up in arms. The mere mention of Mayor Kendrick's name onstage brought a wave of boos and catcalls from the audience. One man was so inflamed he shouted out, "Let's march on the City Hall!"

One speaker after the next extolled Butler's law enforcement leadership, praising him as a "man of destiny" who had come to deliver Philadelphia from its criminal tormentors. The climax of the evening came when the audience, standing as one, passed a resolution in support of Butler, demanding that this "intrepid soldier, fearless officer, and devoted servant of the people be retained until his work is fully completed."

Butler—utterly worn out by the relentless combat of his 18-hour days—was unable to enjoy this dramatic show of public support. He was home in bed, after suffering a recurrence of the severe bronchitis that had been plaguing him since July. The week before, Butler had marched in a rain-drenched parade with an elite Philadelphia police unit to demonstrate that he was not going to quit and run. After returning home, he collapsed in bed. Butler was on the verge of pneumonia, his temperature was spiking at 102, he had lost over 25 pounds from his wiry 158-pound frame, and his breathing and heartbeat were erratic.

In the general's absence, the aroused citizenry of Philadelphia continued to harass Mayor Kendrick on his behalf, deluging the mayor's office with phone calls, letters and telegrams. Three days after the raucous town meeting at the Academy of Music, Kendrick summoned a still-feeble Butler to his office. The general got out of bed and dressed in full

Rum and Rot
in Philadelphia

Gangsters. Bankers. Political bosses. The rampant corruption of the Prohibition years often made it hard to tell them apart. In New York, Mayor Jimmy Walker enjoyed a chummy association with gangland. In Chicago, "Big Bill" Thompson's mayoral reign was thoroughly entwined with the notorious underworld operation of Al Capone. And in Philadelphia, the Vare machine—run by Republican congressman William S. Vare—acted as enforcer and protector for the thriving bootleg rackets.

As long as Vare ruled Philadelphia politics, Smedley Butler charged, there was no way the city could be cleaned up. Under the political strongman's watchful eye, bootleggers reaped fortunes, police precincts were bought off, and banks became lucrative money-laundering machines. The reek of corruption spread throughout the city.

Meanwhile, Vare himself grew more prosperous and powerful. By 1926, the man who began his career peddling vegetables door to door had reached the political heights. He owned three homes—in Philadelphia, Atlantic City and Florida. His machine controlled the state of Pennsylvania. He was a newly elected U.S. senator, after running one of the most lavish campaigns in political history. And two years later, he would be credited with securing the Republican presidential nomination for Herbert Hoover.

Birds of a feather: bootlegger Hoff [above] and GOP boss Vare

But Vare's triumph was short-lived. The Senate refused to seat him, charging that he had bought his election. And in 1928, he suffered a stroke from which he never fully recovered.

In his weakened condition, Vare was unable to block Philadelphia district attorney John Monaghan from launching a mammoth grand jury investigation into city corruption in 1928. By then, Butler was long gone from his public safety post. But the probe, which made sensational headlines for more than a year, proved the general was right when he called Philadelphia a "cesspool."

The grand jury hearing was prompted by a rash of gangland killings in the City of Brotherly Love. (One of the more memorable victims was a hunchbacked dwarf named Hughie McLoon, who had been the mascot for the Philadelphia Athletics baseball team before getting mixed up in bootlegging.) The picture that witnesses painted of Philadelphia was not pretty. In the years since Butler's cleanup campaign, the city had become the main spigot for bootleg liquor in the country, pumping out booze to cities far and wide in bottles labeled "hair oil" and "perfume."

The bootleg baron in charge of this sprawling pipeline was a well-tailored charmer named Max "Boo Boo" Hoff. A small-time boxing promoter, Hoff had worked his way into the booze rackets with stunning success. The hooch mogul enjoyed his newfound wealth, swanning around town with beautiful women and pug-faced bodyguards. He once threw a New Year's Eve party featuring the Broadway star Al Jolson and opened the ballroom doors to anyone who showed up in evening attire. Generous to a fault, Hoff showered bottles of bootleg whiskey and other Christmas gifts on city officials—including Butler's successor as public safety director.

Prosecutor Monaghan called Hoff "a giant spider in the middle of a great web...a man who sees everything, knows everything and controls everything in the underworld." Monaghan hauled Hoff in front of the grand jury eight separate times. But he could never get the goods on him. Boo Boo went to his grave a free man.

uniform, with the help of Ethel, who slipped his big overcoat over his shoulders as he left the house. When he arrived at City Hall, there was a frantic crowd of newspaper reporters, photographers and well-wishers waiting in the corridor outside his office. Butler flopped into his swivel chair with a wheezy sigh.

"God, but I feel rotten," Butler told the press pack. "My legs buckle up as though the knees were loose hinges."

He lit up a cigarette and took a drag, but quickly plucked it from his mouth with a grimace. "Tastes like straw. Nothing at all. This is the first time in my life I'm getting no fun from smoking. Christ, but I feel rotten. But I'm going through with it."

> The RAID on the Ritz sealed Butler's FATE.

Butler then marched unsteadily down the hall to the mayor's office. The showdown lasted one hour. And when the general emerged, he was victorious. With the public's ardent support, he had held on to his job. And, Butler made clear, he would continue to rock the boat.

The day after his meeting with the mayor, Butler addressed his inspectors and lieutenants. He was in a philosophical mood. He promised that he was through with cussing them. "No more profanity from me. It's a useless thing, doesn't add force to anything that is said." Besides, he added, his fits of profane anger were bad for his health. Between the poisonous politics of City Hall and his failing health, he told his men, he didn't know how long he could hold on to his police command. But he urged them to keep fighting for their city.

"I may die or go away, but carry on. That's the only real thing in life. Stick to what you know is right. Make the crooks fear you. Don't be afraid of anything."

Then, with a sad shake of his head, he told his men that he had just heard about a cop who was caught trying to bribe one of the Phillies. *The Phillies!*

"Don't let anybody get you. Don't go crooked for anybody. Keep your eyes open and your conscience clean. Keep your badge bright and clean. Think of that badge as the outward symbol of your honor. That's the way I think of it. And when you see anything crooked, raise the dickens."

His thin, pale face broke into a wide grin. "You see? I'm saying dickens."

His men had heard Butler's inspirational talks before. But they took this one to heart. Commanders like this didn't come along very often—men who actually believed that justice could prevail. Butler's brass wanted to savor their days with him. They were street-smart enough to know those days were numbered.

EARLY MORNING, DECEMBER 3, 1925

Shortly after midnight, a squad of Butler's men burst into the ballroom of the Ritz-Carlton Hotel, led by Magistrate Edward P. Carney. "You're all under arrest!" bellowed Carney, sending the elegantly dressed, intoxicated revelers scrambling madly for the doors. Women abandoned their fur wraps, men left behind their cashmere overcoats. One grand dame was so soused that not even the police could budge her. "You're a flapper-chaser," she snarled at Carney, sprawling precariously in her chair.

While some of the cops confiscated bottles of Scotch and champagne and loaded the swells into paddy wagons, others sprinted upstairs to a suite where the hosts of the party—Mr. and Mrs. John Barnes—were presiding over a well-lubricated private soiree. Couples staggered from the room, gulping highballs and tossing the glasses on the floor. Inside, several gentlemen in tuxedos were howling barbershop songs at the top of their lungs, while propping each other up. Girls as young as 16 and 17 were being fed cocktails by their escorts. Host John Barnes was a wealthy coal magnate and a club man in good standing. But his rooms stank like a common saloon, one cop later said.

Eddie Carney, a tough Irish judge who had won his seat in defiance of the Vare machine, had a tempestuous history with Butler. Carney had accused Butler of not pursuing the rich and powerful as aggressively as he said he would. City Hall reporters once had to jump in between the two men to keep them from coming to blows in Butler's office.

But the morning after the Ritz-Carlton raid, the two men were all smiles as they relived the operation with the press. Butler, who had long complained that municipal judges were undermining his crime crackdown, had finally found an ally as fearless as he was. "Eddie," said Butler, draping his arm

BRIGADIER GENERAL
SMEDLEY D. BUTLER
UNITED STATES MARINE CORPS

DIRECTOR OF
PUBLIC SAFETY
PHILADELPHIA
JANUARY 7, 1924
DECEMBER 23, 1925

HE ENFORCED THE LAW IMPARTIALLY
HE DEFENDED IT COURAGEOUSLY
HE PROVED INCORRUPTIBLE

AFTER BUTLER WAS FIRED, THE CITY PUT UP A PLAQUE IN HIS HONOR, BUT HE WAS UNIMPRESSED

around the militant magistrate, "we're going to padlock the entire Ritz-Carlton. Something must be done to teach these big fellows that they must obey the law as well as the little fellows."

Ever since the humiliating night of the Bal Masque, the Ritz had loomed as a symbol of wealthy arrogance and lawlessness to Butler. "I call it a disgrace, and I believe the American people would see the Ritz-Carlton torn down stone by stone rather than allow such conditions to go on. I am going to make an issue of it and see if the people of Philadelphia will stand back of me."

But the Ritz-Carlton raid would be Butler's final stand. City high-hats, many of whom had attended the Barnes party, came after Butler with all their might.

Philadelphia's establishment made it clear to Mayor Kendrick that Butler had to go.

Butler did not go quietly. After Kendrick fired him, he stirred up a tempest in the press, savaging the mayor as a "weak fish" and a tool of "the gang" of thieves who ran Philadelphia. As Butler was leaving City Hall for the final time, swarmed by reporters and aides, one of the political hacks who hacks who was eagerly awaiting his departure began heckling the general. A cop in motorcycle boots pushed his way through the throng and sent the heckler sprawling with one punch. To the very end, an air of combat swirled around Butler's tenure.

A few days after his departure from Philadelphia, Butler gave a speech in Pittsburgh's Soldiers Memorial Hall about his tumultuous stint as a crime fighter. He was wearing his marine uniform again. The audience was filled with many veterans, some of whom he recognized and made a point of saluting.

He was no reformer, Butler told the audience that night, he was a soldier. And it was time to fight like a soldier for democracy. "Until people get mad, you can't get anywhere. I want to impress on you that this is not a pacifist movement." If you want to save democracy from corruption, the general shouted, "You've got to be belligerent!" And the crowd cheered him until they were hoarse.

Smedley Butler's war had just begun.

BUTLER "QUITS" TODAY WITH PARTING BLAST AT WIDE OPEN TOWN

WON'T RESIGN, MUST BE FIRED, HIS ULTIMATUM

Resents "Stunning Blow" After "Suicidal Sacrifice" But Will Bow to Mayor's Order for His Suspension

At noon today General Smedley D. Butler will "leave" the office of Director of Public Safety, in conformity with Mayor Kendrick's order.

General Butler's assistant and successor, George W. Elliott, will assume charge at that hour.

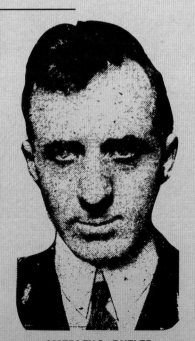

SMEDLEY D. BUTLER

General Butler, after resigning from the Marine Corps, faces dismissal from his post of Director of Public Safety by Mayor Kendrick. General Butler refused to resign his local post, as demanded by the Mayor, and has asked the latter to give reasons for his dismissal.

BUTLER REVEALED AN EXPLOSIVE STORY ABOUT ITALIAN FASCIST DICTATOR, MUSSOLINI, TOLD BY NEWSPAPERMAN CORNELIUS VANDERBILT.

WOULD YOU LIKE TO SEE MY ITALY, MR. VANDERBILT?

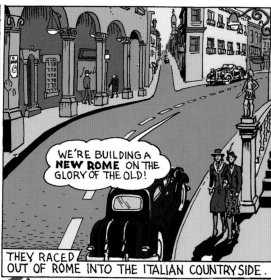

WE'RE BUILDING A **NEW ROME** ON THE GLORY OF THE OLD!

THEY RACED OUT OF ROME INTO THE ITALIAN COUNTRYSIDE.

WOMF

YOU JUST KILLED THAT LITTLE GIRL!

NEVER LOOK BACK, MR. VANDERBILT, NEVER LOOK BACK IN LIFE.

SIENA 138 KM

110

Act 6

Washington Is
Burning

MARINE CORPS BASE, QUANTICO, VIRGINIA, JANUARY 1931

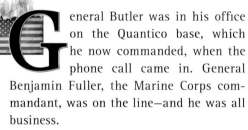eneral Butler was in his office on the Quantico base, which he now commanded, when the phone call came in. General Benjamin Fuller, the Marine Corps commandant, was on the line—and he was all business.

"General Butler, you are hereby placed under arrest to await trial by general court-martial. You will turn over your command to your next senior, General Berkeley, and you will be restricted to the limits of your post. The secretary of the navy wishes you to know that this action is taken by the direct personal order of the president of the United States."

Not yet 50, Butler was the youngest major general in the U.S. armed forces, and the most decorated marine in American history. But now he was making military history of a different kind—he was the first senior officer since the Civil War to be placed under arrest.

And it was Ben Fuller, of all people, who was slapping him in irons. Butler should have been sitting in Fuller's armchair at the War Department. As the senior ranking officer in the Marine Corps, Butler had been in line to be the next USMC commandant. But the legendary general had never played by Washington's rules, had never courted the swivel-chair admirals back in the War Department. When it came time for Butler to be handed the ultimate prize for his decades of heroic service, the corps had passed over him, digging deeply into the officers' ranks and giving the top post to the obscure General Fuller instead.

By 1931, Smedley Butler was a solitary gladiator in the Washington political arena. In May 1928, his father, the powerful Congressman Thomas S. Butler—builder of fleets, maker of kings—had died of heart disease in his Washington apartment. Stationed overseas in China at the time, on his final imperial mission, General Butler could not even see his father laid to rest.

The man whom Butler addressed in letters as "Daddy" to the very end was no longer there to look out for him.

Now Butler was a man in full, and fully on his own. He began taking more risks. Even if he was going to be punished for his independent streak, he was going to let his colors fly. Never one to bite his tongue, Butler became increasingly outspoken, and it made him no friends in the nation's capital. He had already been reprimanded for telling the truth about the U.S. occupation of Nicaragua. During a speech in Pittsburgh, the straight-shooting general revealed his role in fixing the 1912 presidential elections. "We marines took charge of two elections in Nicaragua. The fellow we had in there nobody liked, but he was a useful fellow—to us—so we declared the opposition candidates bandits. Four hundred natives were found who would vote for the proper candidate… [They] were assembled in line and when they had voted, the polls were closed."

In January 1931, Butler ignited an even bigger explosion—big enough to cause an international incident and get him arrested. During a speech on war and peace before the Philadelphia Contemporary Club, Butler declared that even though he condemned war, he did not advocate disarmament because some "mad-dog nations" could not be trusted. To illustrate his point, he told a shocking story about Benito Mussolini, the flamboyant

UNITED STATES APOLOGIZES TO MUSSOLINI; GENERAL BUTLER TO BE COURT-MARTIALED FOR SLUR ON ITALIAN PREMIER IN SPEECH

'REGRET' VOICED TO ROME

Steps Taken by Stimson and Adams Said to Be on Hoover's Decision

MARINE HEAD UNDER ARREST

Italian Press Calls Speech "Impudent," but Officials Consider Incident Closed

WASHINGTON, Jan. 29.—The United States Government apologized today to Benito Mussolini, Dictator of Italy, for the "reflections" upon him contained in the speech of Major Gen. Smedley Butler of the Marine Corps at Philadelphia, Jan. 19, in which General Butler had referred to the Italian Premier as a hit-and-run driver.

fascist who had set himself up as Rome's modern Caesar. Until then, the squat dictator enjoyed an adoring press in America, particularly in press baron Henry Luce's *Time* and *Fortune* magazines. "The moral force of Fascism," Luce announced, "may be the inspiration for the next general march of mankind." But the story Butler related in Philadelphia portrayed Mussolini as a moral degenerate.

One day, Butler recounted, Mussolini invited an American visitor to accompany him on a road tour of Italy. Jumping into his custom-designed Fiat—a roadster equipped with an armored nose to plow through fences and barbed wire—Mussolini and his guest roared out of Rome, with sirens blaring to stop traffic, and zoomed down the Via Veneto. For the next three days, Il Duce showed off his country to his American passenger, racing at hair-raising speeds down to Naples, then up through the Italian Riviera and finally down the spine of the Apennines back to Rome. As Mussolini gunned his armored racecar through the countryside, he scattered donkeys and bicycle riders and shuffling priests in his path, missing many pedestrians by inches.

On the final afternoon, as Mussolini motored recklessly through a small village called San Quirito, it finally happened. A little girl suddenly sprinted into his path. Mussolini's heavy vehicle instantly crushed

MUSSOLINI WAS GIVEN THE CELEBRITY TREATMENT.

the child. But the dictator did not even slow down. As the American passenger screamed in horror and whipped around to see the tiny crumpled-up form in the road, he felt Mussolini's hand on his knee. "Never look back," Il Duce said, "never look back in life."

A couple of hours later, back in his Rome palace, Mussolini sat down to dinner with his visitor as if nothing had happened, gorging on cold chicken in gelatin, cold salmon, mussels and steaming bowls of spaghetti.

After Butler's stunning speech, the Italian government flew into a frenzy. Mussolini flatly denied the story, stating, "I have never taken an American on a motor-car trip around Italy, neither have I run over a child, man or woman." In Washington, the Hoover administration reacted with surprising vehemence, issuing an abject apology to Mussolini for General Butler's "discourteous and unwarranted utterances," and ordering Butler's immediate arrest.

Butler was confined to his quarters at Quantico, 36 miles down the Potomac from Washington. The general had helped carve the sprawling base out of the Virginia swampland, turning it into a center of advanced military training and education for the marines. But now—staring out the window of his whitewashed clapboard house, as a marine guard hauled down the command flag on his lawn—Butler felt the deepest humiliation of his life. After "33 years with a spotless record"—including two Medals of Honor—he was being treated like a squalid criminal. "It was a pretty savage blow."

One afternoon while preparing his defense, Butler was visited at home by a junior officer. The general told the young officer that President Hoover had an ulterior motive for punishing him so harshly. During the Boxer Rebellion, Butler said, as his marine regiment was fighting to lift the siege of Tientsin, they were disgusted to find an American engineer hiding in the basement with the women and children. The marines dragged the coward from the hideout and roughed him up, forcing him to take up duty on the city wall. "Do you know who that man was?" Butler asked his visitor. "Herbert Hoover."

Butler's arrest set off a nationwide outcry. Theater crowds cheered when the scrappy, iconic general appeared in newsreels, and booed pictures of Mussolini and Hoover's secretary of state, Henry Stimson, who had pushed for tough treatment of Butler. Franklin Roosevelt, then governor of New York, offered to help Butler find top legal counsel. When Butler procured the services of Washington attorney Henry Leonard—a retired marine major who had lost an arm in the battle of Tientsin—Hoover must have seen this as

HOOVER HAD A SECRET REASON FOR TARGETING BUTLER.

a well-aimed shot from the military men across his bow.

Letters of support poured in to Butler, and the White House was flooded with angry tirades. "What has come over the Republican administration, that they should break their necks to apologize to this autocrat, [a man] who should have been put on trial himself, instead of our own great General Butler," wrote one citizen. "I condemn this toadying to European despots as being un-American."

What's next, wrote another—were Hoover and Stimson going to order Butler to "apologize to Al Capone?"

Meanwhile, as more evidence of Mussolini's road mayhem began to surface, the dictator's denials grew shakier. Il Duce's American passenger came forward to corroborate the story. He turned out to be globetrotting newspaperman and son of fortune Cornelius Vanderbilt, Jr., who showed Secretary of State Stimson a photograph that Mussolini had signed to commemorate their "pleasant weekend" and other memorabilia from their fatal road trip. The Italian government was forced to concede that Mussolini had entertained Vanderbilt—and, behind the scenes, the dictator's minions pressed the Hoover administration to put the matter to rest before it got any messier.

President Hoover, unnerved by the growing public relations disaster, canceled Butler's court-martial on February 9. The administration wanted Butler to apologize to Mussolini, but he adamantly refused. In the end, Hoover gave the unbending general a mild reprimand and restored him to his command with full rank and privileges.

It was a resounding victory for the general. He had stood up to a brutal dictator—and the dictator's appeasers in Washington—and had forced them to back down.

Butler's reputation as a fighting man—not just in overseas wars but in domestic ones—kept growing. Will Rogers, America's wit and conscience, marveled, "I was glad to see Smedley Butler get out of his case as he did. You know that fellow just belongs in war all the time…He will fight anybody, any time…I do admire him."

No Americans admired Butler more than veterans. They followed him in peace as they had in war. After the general faced down Mussolini and Hoover, he received a heartfelt letter from a Los Angeles veteran

OFFICIALS SILENT AS GENERAL BUTLER IS FREED

It's All Over Now!

Major General Smedley D. Butler, native son of West Chester, won't have to face trial after all. Court martial charges against him have been called off by Secretary of the Navy Charles F. Adams.

INCIDENT NOW REGARDED AS CLOSED

Marine Chief Expresses Regrets to Naval Head; Reprimand Is Delivered to Him

Washington (UP)—The Butler-Mussolini incident was apparently a closed chapter to-day with all figures concerned declining further enlightenment on its abrupt ending.

The general court martial of Major General Smedley D. Butler, scheduled to begin Monday in Phil-

who had been gassed in the World War. "I was mighty pleased to read in the newspapers that you had been completely vindicated and most important of all that you did not apologize," he wrote. "Life is too short for an old soldier like you to lower your standard and honor at any time... When you finally pass on as we all will, you will have the satisfaction of knowing that you will be remembered as the man who never backed down."

America's veterans would soon call on Butler to fight another great battle.

WASHINGTON, D.C., JULY 1932

Smedley Butler stood on the makeshift platform in the glaring sun, squinting out at the vast army arrayed before him. It was a ragged force, more than 15,000 strong—weather-beaten men and women in tattered clothes crowded between tents and shacks, and scrawny kids playing in the mud holes left over from the summer rain.

The scruffy army had descended upon Washington, D.C., from cities and hamlets all over the nation, desperate veterans of the Great War and their hungry families, hopping freight trains and hitching rides to press their case in the nation's capital. The newspapers and newsreels called them the Bonus Army, but the former soldiers said they weren't looking for any special favors from Congress. They just wanted compensation for the wages they lost when they were sent to the Western Front, where they had risked their lives for just a dollar a day.

It was the hardest of times. Like half the country, the assembled vets were out of work or not getting a full paycheck. President Hoover said the Depression wasn't that bad. "Nobody is actually starving," the round-faced chief executive insisted. But many of the families packed into the Hooverville camp along the banks of Washington's muddy Anacostia River *were* hungry. During their siege, the vets had gathered on the Capitol lawn to serenade Congress with their own bitter version of

A **RAGGED** ARMY OF **VETERANS** SET UP CAMP IN **WASHINGTON** WITH THEIR FAMILIES.

"Over There"—*The Yanks are starving, the yanks are starving everywhere.*

The Bonus Army camp was a model of military discipline and ingenuity. The veterans' ramshackle barracks were neatly tended and American flags flew everywhere in the camp. A library was set up inside a big Salvation Army tent, and boxing matches and stage shows were organized for entertainment. Music floated through the air—gospel, blues, country and popular tunes—as singers and guitar pluckers found one another.

Unlike the ranks of the U.S. military, the camp was racially integrated. Blacks and whites shared meals, chores and decision making—a state of affairs that deeply unnerved the Hoover administration and its war officials when they found out.

Despite the Bonus Army's solidarity, after weeks of marching and lobbying, they still failed to sway Washington. Hoover remained adamantly opposed to the Bonus Bill—veterans would simply "waste" their government payments, he argued, so the bill would not work as an economic stimulus. And in June, Hoover's Republican majority in the Senate soundly defeated the bill.

Afraid that the Bonus Army would grow demoralized and begin to drift away, its leaders reached out to a man they knew would inspire the vets—Smedley Butler. The general quickly agreed to address the Bonus troops. After spending his entire adult life in the marines, old Devil Dog

had retired from the corps in September 1931, with a parting shot at the brass. Butler knew that the Mussolini fracas had sounded taps for his military career. He announced that he was retiring so that he could fully speak his mind, vowing that he would tell the powerful people who "abuse" our soldiers "where the hell to get off."

The vocal general made it clear that chief among his targets would be the "war racketeers" who reaped extravagant profits from America's military adventures, while men like those encamped in Washington worried about their next meal. Some of these war profiteers—like Pierre S. DuPont, whose family's chemical company made a fortune during the World War—had the nerve to lobby against the veterans' payments, declaring that the Bonus Bill would make "mercenaries out of our patriotic boys." Other death merchants claimed that many of the Bonus Army marchers were really bums and scam artists.

By the time Butler climbed onstage in the Bonus Army camp, he was seething with outrage over the treatment of America's former fighting men. Ever since he had announced his post-retirement plan to help America's veterans, he had been barraged with plaintive letters from former soldiers, including many who had served under him, and their mothers and widows. They asked Butler for help finding jobs or winning disability payments or simply for a $5 handout to get them through the month. "We Marines have always looked

PIERRE DUPONT, WAR PROFITEER

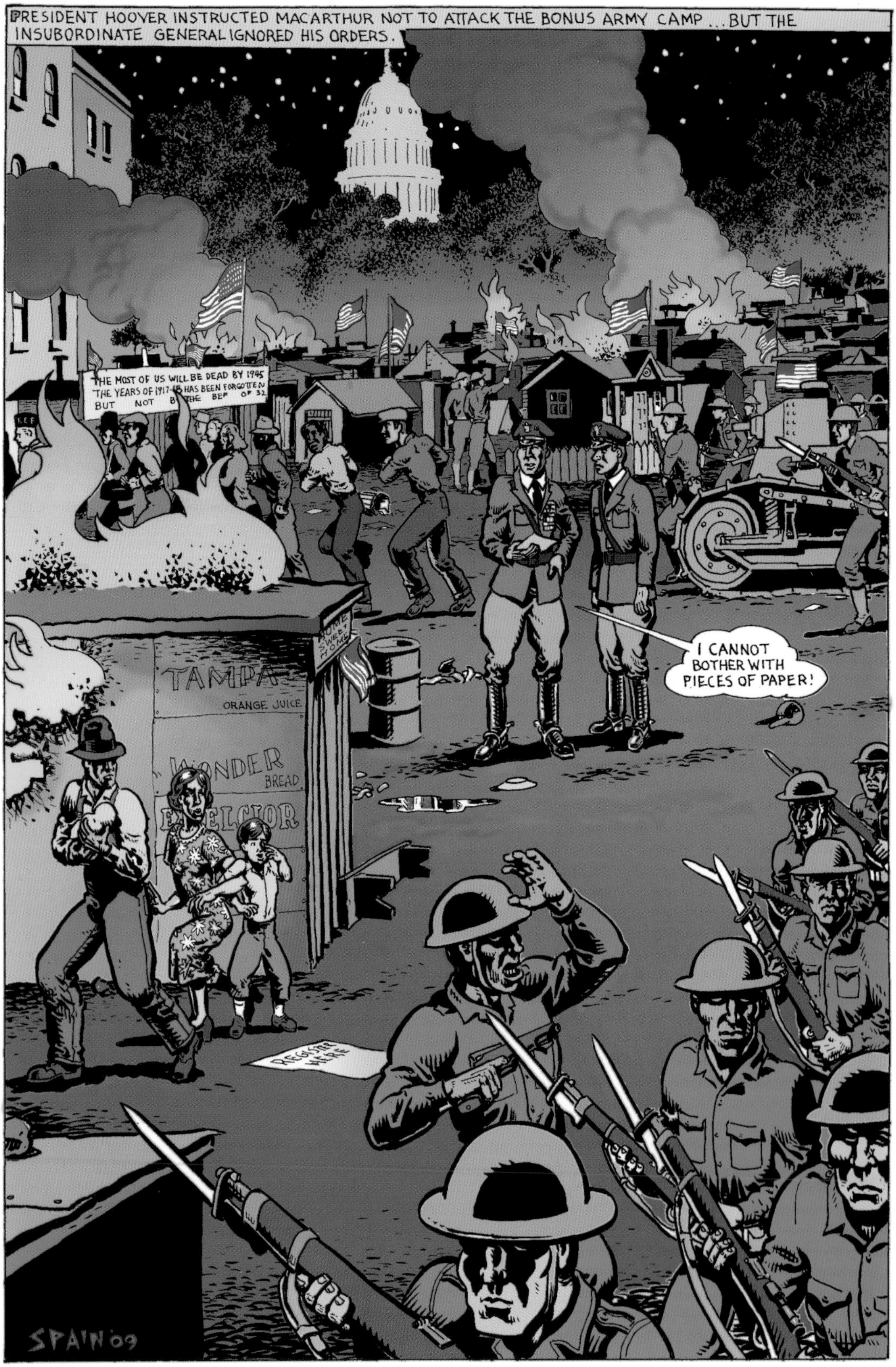
PRESIDENT HOOVER INSTRUCTED MACARTHUR NOT TO ATTACK THE BONUS ARMY CAMP ... BUT THE INSUBORDINATE GENERAL IGNORED HIS ORDERS.
THE MOST OF US WILL BE DEAD BY 1945
THE YEARS OF 1917- HAS BEEN FORGOTTEN
BUT NOT B THE BEF OF 32
HOME SWEET HOME
TAMPA
ORANGE JUICE
WONDER
BREAD
I CANNOT BOTHER WITH PIECES OF PAPER!
REGISTER HERE
SPAIN '09

to you as an Uncle, some one to tell our troubles to, or request favors of," wrote one unemployed vet from Maryland.

The letters, unfailingly polite and respectful even in their raw desperation, were a heartbreaking window into the suffering of Depression America. "Dear Sir," wrote a Pennsylvania marine who had been forced to leave the corps to take care of his ailing wife and baby, "I am in need of a job of some kind very bad. I am willing to do any thing so I can keep my family together, keep them from starving."

The mother of two boys who had served on the Western Front told Butler that he was her family's last hope. "I am a Widdow, got a son killed in France in 1918 and another one all shot to pieces, I mean health no good gassed wounded and a little shell shocked as nervous as can be and sickly not able to make his own living...Mr. Butler my Son and myself are undernourished and many a day we were so hungery didn't know what to do for food."

Now Butler stood looking at a vast throng of these suffering veterans and their families. The blazing sun was starting to set and the sky was turning crimson. The crowd, hushed and patient in the daylight's final fury, bent towards him. "Soldiers lean to the Generals whose hearts beat in unison with theirs," as one vet had written the general.

Butler threw off his coat and began to speak, his famous growl of a voice thrumming with feeling. "You hear folks call you fellows tramps—but they didn't call you that in '17 and '18!" he shouted. "I never saw such fine soldiers. I never saw such discipline...I consider it an honor to be asked to speak to you."

Clouds of smoke and TEAR GAS drifted over the capital.

Butler urged the Bonus troops to stand their ground in Washington until they won passage of their bill. "If you don't hang together, you aren't worth a damn!" He was their general again, his wiry frame electric with motion, his blue shirt drenched in sweat. "You have as much right to lobby here as the United States Steel Corporation!"

If some veterans had to return home, Butler told the crowd, they should stay politically mobilized. "When you get home, go to the polls in November and lick the hell out of those who are against you," he roared. "You know who they are...Now go to it!"

Afterwards, the soldiers mobbed Butler. Many had served with him in China, the Philippines, Haiti, Nicaragua, France. Butler had brought his son, 23-year-old Smedley, Jr., to see these battered warriors in person. They too were his sons. Butler stayed up late into the night talking to the veterans around a campfire, listening to their tragic stories. In the morning, he breakfasted on potatoes, hard bread and coffee with the vets. Before returning to his new home in Newtown Square, a small town outside Philadelphia, Butler urged the Bonus soldiers to stay peaceful.

"You're all right so long as you keep your sense of humor. If you slip into lawlessness of any kind, you will lose the sympathy of 120 million people in the nation." But it was President Hoover and his military aides who would bring a violent end to the Bonus Army's courageous saga.

An eye-stinging blue mist drifted over downtown Washington. Columns of steel-helmeted soldiers in gas masks were trotting down Pennsylvania and

FDR CALLED GENERAL MACARTHUR "A POTENTIAL MUSSOLINI."

But the man leading the military's charge—General Douglas MacArthur, the already fabled army chief of staff—showed no mercy, even though some of the men he was hunting down that day had fought for him in the Great War. MacArthur seemed to glory in his vicious rout of the veterans. He was known for his love of military regalia, storming onto the battlefields of France in rakish scarves and high boots and brandishing a riding crop. Off-duty, he was fond of wearing lushly colored kimonos and smoking cigarettes in a jeweled holder. In Washington that day, MacArthur strutted down the streets in full dress uniform, jodhpurs and all, as if to lord his authority over the scraggly veterans.

If Smedley Butler was a soldier's general—the kind who would join a doughboy in the chow line or carry his rucksack—Douglas MacArthur was the very epitome of the imperial general. Butler couldn't stand his fellow war hero; he thought he was a stuffed shirt and an elitist. MacArthur was brilliant, vain, fearless, half-mad. He erected a huge mirror behind his office desk to heighten his stature and took to speaking of himself in the third person, like an Oriental despot. ("The General will have his tea now.") And he didn't like taking orders, not even from his commander in chief.

Hoover ordered MacArthur to halt his charge at the Anacostia River, before reaching the Bonus Army camp, fearing the newspaper headlines if veterans or their family members became casualties. But the general simply pretended he never received the president's instructions. Instead, as night fell over the capital,

Constitution avenues, firing rounds of tear gas and jabbing with their bayonets at anyone too slow to get out of the way. The foot soldiers were reinforced by cavalry units with glinting sabers, machine gunners and rumbling tanks. President Hoover had unleashed the full might of the U.S. military on the Bonus Army.

The vets, choking on gas and scattering in retreat, could not believe that American troops had taken the field against them. They were too stunned to fight back. It seemed like a nightmarish echo of the chaos on the Western Front. A large black veteran climbed up a tree and began waving an American flag, as if to remind the advancing troops whom they were attacking. In a voice as deeply forlorn as a gospel singer's, the vet chanted, "God that gave us this here country, help us now."

he sent his troops storming across the Anacostia Bridge to set ablaze the veterans' tents and shacks.

Women with babies ran screaming from the inferno. "Let's get the hell out of here," a vet yelled to his two young sons, "they're going to kill us all." Residents in the surrounding black neighborhood—where the drifting tear gas was also choking people—offered sanctuary to the fleeing families.

Just blocks away, Hoover stared out the second floor of the White House as the flames danced madly in the night sky, and then went to bed. He had been taking sedatives during the Bonus Army siege of Washington to help him sleep.

Meanwhile, MacArthur seemed to take charge of the government. Back at his headquarters, during a bizarre press conference that stretched past midnight, he belligerently defended his insubordinate actions by claiming the Bonus Army was made up of communists and criminals, not war veterans. "The mob," as he called the veterans, "were animated by the spirit of revolution."

MacArthur and his equally paranoid comrade—Brigadier General George Van Horn Moseley, the army's intelligence chief—had convinced themselves that the veterans' pilgrimage was part of a nefarious plot to overthrow the United States government. A MacArthur aide claimed to have found "a secret document" that revealed a "Communist plan" to seize Washington and hang senior officials in front of the Capitol. "At the very top of the list was Army Chief of Staff MacArthur," the general's aide gravely announced.

The next morning, clouds of smoke from the burned-out camp were still wafting

BEATEN AND **GASSED,** THE **BONUS ARMY** MARCHERS FLED **WASHINGTON.**

over the Capitol dome. The newspapers were filled with pitiful accounts of the Bonus Army rout. Streams of refugees, including mothers with hacking infants, trudged through an early morning rain across the Maryland border, not knowing where to go. Propped up in bed at Hyde Park and reading the shocking newspaper reports, Franklin Roosevelt–the Democratic nominee for president–shook his head in dismay. "They must be camping right now alongside the roads out of Washington," FDR told his aide Rex Tugwell. "And some of them have families. It is a wonder there isn't more resentment, more radicalism, when people are treated that way."

What Hoover should have done, FDR continued, was to send out for coffee and sandwiches and sit down with the leaders of the Bonus Army. Instead, he let MacArthur and his stormtroopers "do their thing."

"MacArthur has just prevented Hoover's reelection," FDR told Tugwell. The insubordinate general made Hoover look like "there is nothing inside the man but jelly."

FDR was clearly disturbed by MacArthur's authoritarian posturing, calling him "the most dangerous man in this country."

"You saw how he strutted down Pennsylvania Avenue," Roosevelt told Tugwell. "You saw that picture of him in the *Times* after the troops chased all those vets out with tear gas and burned their shelters. Did you ever see anyone more self-satisfied? There's a potential Mussolini for you. Right here at home."

Franklin Roosevelt was not the only one outraged by the assault on the Bonus Army. For Smedley Butler, it was the final blow against the tattered dignity of the American fighting man.

The former soldier was from a long line of Republicans. But because of the Hoover administration's disgraceful actions, Butler announced he was switching sides. He could not support a government that "used gas and bayonets on unarmed human beings."

"No one has any business occupying the White House who doesn't love his own people," he declared.

The week after Hoover scattered the Bonus Army, Butler wrote to Franklin Roosevelt, offering to help his presidential campaign in any way he could. "I am convinced we are in a most critical condition in this Country and that your candidacy and platform offer the only real chance for salvation. If I can be of service, please send the order along."

BUTLER THREW HIMSELF INTO FDR'S CAMPAIGN.

Roosevelt enlisted the former general as a campaign speaker, sending him to veterans' rallies, where he stumped passionately for the Democratic candidate. For Butler, it would be the greatest battle of his life—the battle for American democracy. The struggle would not end in November, with FDR's sweeping triumph over Hoover. It would come to a climax during Roosevelt's first term, in a showdown that pitted Butler against some of the most powerful forces in the country.

By then, the soldier was just a citizen—living with his wife in a modest bungalow that was stuffed with the memorabilia of a lifetime of military service, and trying to make ends meet as a speaker and writer. But Smedley Butler would show how formidable a citizen can be in the defense of his country.

He spoke at Veterans of Foreign Wars gatherings; Kiwanis, Elks and Rotary Clubs; Gold Star Mothers Clubs; Chambers of Commerce luncheons; B'Nai Brith meetings and a Jewish Basketball League banquet. Everyone wanted to hear the legendary, straight-shooting military hero, from black servicemen's organizations to Ku Klux Klan chapters. During 1932, the man billed as "America's Most Colorful Soldier" went on a 100,000-mile coast-to-coast speaking tour. His normal speaking fee was $150, but he charged veterans' groups just $50. He pledged to donate half his income from

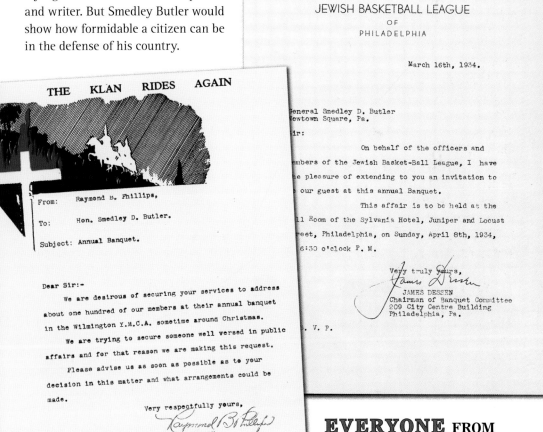

EVERYONE FROM THE **KKK** TO **JEWISH** ATHLETIC GROUPS WANTED HIM TO SPEAK.

speaking and writing to the unemployed, even though money was a constant worry for him and Ethel, and they had no other major source of income. Butler was not the type of retired general whom war manufacturers put on their boards.

He didn't like flying—being up in the air made the old foot soldier nervous. So he asked his speakers bureau to book him on trains whenever possible. He logged so many miles on the tracks that Union Pacific asked him to do a testimonial for its Portland Rose line between Chicago and the Pacific Northwest.

Public speeches were boxing matches for the combative Butler. Onstage, he danced from one foot to the other, swinging at the air with clenched fists like he was knocking the daylights out of his enemies. He worked himself until he dropped. Isabel Darlington, his aunt and lawyer, periodically wrote his bureau that he was being pushed over the edge. "His health is breaking down," she warned in one letter. At an event in Portland, where his microphone sputtered in and out, Butler was forced to shout so loudly that "he suffered a rupture."

No one pushed Butler harder than himself. After his long years overseas, he was not only getting to know his country again—he was delivering a message to his fellow citizens that he knew they must hear. Decades before another general, Dwight Eisenhower, warned the country about the dangerous power of "the military-industrial complex," Butler was alerting America that "war is a racket." And the biggest racketeers, he told his audiences, were the Washington politicians, Wall Street banks, oil companies and weapons merchants that profited from the blood and misery of war.

Butler told soldiers to stop being "suckers." The real war, he declared, "is between you veterans—four or five million of you—and all the lying, over-stuffed, sleek and slippery customers who send soldiers off to war with cheers and welcome them home again—what's left of 'em—with kicks! It's war with that little, tight, close-fisted bunch of Tories who think that God made the United States for about

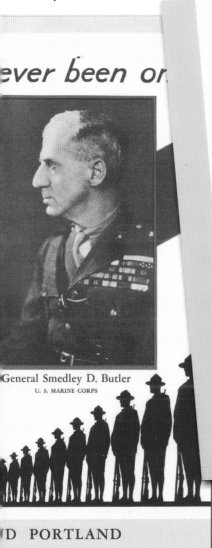

General Smedley D. Butler
U. S. MARINE CORPS

...ever been or...

D PORTLAND

A Bouquet from the General

UNION PACIFIC SYSTEM OVERLAND

BUTLER SPENT **SO MUCH TIME** ON TRAINS, **U**NION **P**ACIFIC FEATURED HIM IN AN AD.

Victory
for the Veterans

Despite his sharp criticism of President Hoover's brutal treatment of the Bonus Army, FDR continued to block the Bonus Bill after he became president. Roosevelt, grappling with the massive misery of the Depression, opposed the giveaway because he thought it extended preferential treatment to one group of Americans. In January 1936, however, Congress voted overwhelmingly to override Roosevelt's veto, and the Bonus Bill finally became law.

On June 16, government checks totaling nearly $2 billion were mailed to more than 3.5 million veterans. The cash infusion gave many hard-hit communities an immediate lift, with veterans rushing out to buy everything from new shoes for their children to new cars.

Roosevelt learned from the traumatic saga of the Bonus Army. On June 22, 1944, as American troops were helping to liberate Europe, the president signed the historic GI Bill of Rights. Soldiers returning from the Second World War would not have to take to the streets after they returned home.

The GI Bill was a wild success, helping build a new American middle class. More than half of the 15 million soldiers who served in the war took advantage of the bill's schooling opportunities or home loans. The bill produced 450,000 engineers, 238,000 teachers, 91,000 scientists and 67,000 doctors. Of the 13 million new houses built in the 1950s, 11 million were financed by GI Bill loans.

This generation of veterans owed its good fortune to the ragged army that descended on Washington during the final year of the Hoover presidency, and kept up the pressure through much of Roosevelt's reign.

two hundred of them and created the rest of us to make their money for them and guard it from foreign danger and lie down in the mud or jump through hoops or do anything else under heaven they want us to do."

Butler was sounding increasingly radical, but his words had more punch than those of the soapbox lefties on the corner, because he was—and continued to be—a decorated American patriot. And he was just getting warmed up.

In 1935, the retired general offered a stunning mea culpa in the pages of a left-wing magazine called *Common Sense.* "I spent 33 years and four months in active military service and during that period I spent most of my time as a high class muscle man for Big Business, for Wall Street and the bankers. In short, I was a racketeer, a gangster for capitalism. I helped make Mexico...safe for American oil interests. I helped make Haiti and Cuba a decent place for the National City Bank boys to collect revenues in. I helped in the raping of a dozen Central American republics for the benefit of Wall Street. I helped purify Nicaragua for the International Banking House of Brown Brothers in 1902–1912. I brought light to the Dominican Republic for the American sugar interests in 1916. I helped make Honduras right for the American fruit companies in 1903. In China in 1927 I helped see to it that Standard Oil went on its way unmolested... Looking back on it, I feel I might have given Al Capone a few hints. The best he could do was to operate in three city districts. We Marines operated on three *continents*."

It was a painfully honest assessment of his military career. And that same year, Butler fired another broadside with a scorching pamphlet titled *War Is a Racket*. The next time America goes to war, Butler argued, it should be fought by the rich and powerful. The World War had minted over 20,000 new millionaires and billionaires, he acidly observed. "How many of these war millionaires shouldered a rifle? How many of them dug a trench? How many of them knew what it meant to go hungry in a rat-infested dugout? How many of them spent sleepless, frightened nights, ducking shells and shrapnel and machine-gun bullets? How many of them parried the bayonet thrust of an enemy? How many of them were wounded or killed in battle?"

Smedley Butler was a man on fire. As he crisscrossed the country speaking about war and peace, and the rights of soldiers, Butler even lit a blowtorch under his old comrade Franklin Roosevelt. It was time for FDR to sign the Bonus Bill—even good presidents needed to be prodded. "You will have to frighten him," Butler told veterans. "Hold a club over his head and he'll sign it, as he will need your votes in 1936."

Butler's barnstorming tour of America electrified his audiences of veterans and jobless workers. But there was one group of men that watched the Butler spectacle with particular interest. They were some of the richest and most powerful figures in the country, and they didn't much care for Butler's heated talk about the "Tory menace." But they were intrigued by the spell he seemed to cast over crowds of disgruntled veterans, and their imaginations raced when the general spoke of holding a club over Franklin Roosevelt's head. Maybe they could enlist the fiery general in their shadowy plot against the Roosevelt administration.

So begins the stunning climax of Butler's saga.

WAR IS A RACKET

GENERAL SMEDLEY D. BUTLER

HIS ANTIWAR **PASSIONS** ERUPTED IN A **1935** BOOK.

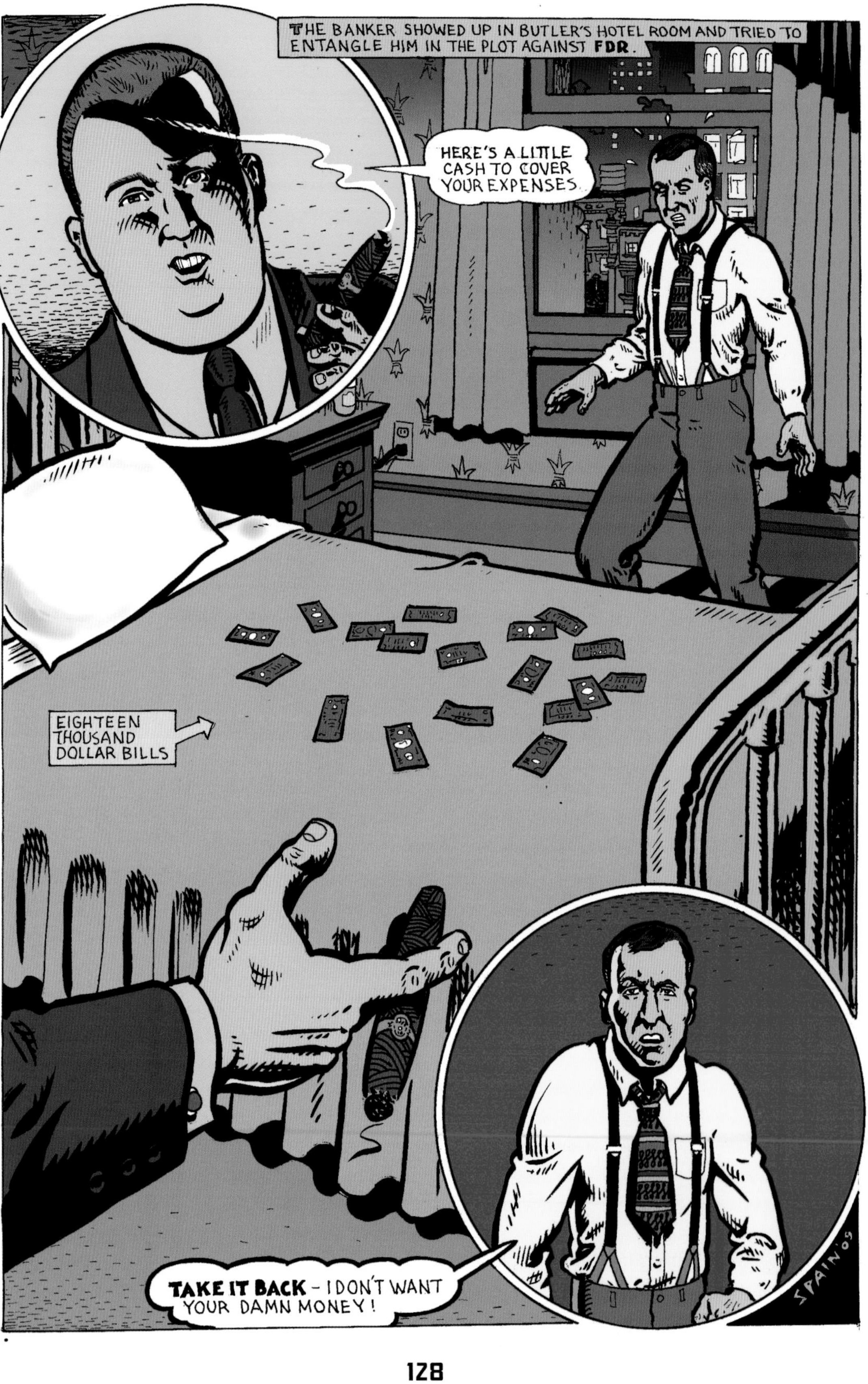
THE BANKER SHOWED UP IN BUTLER'S HOTEL ROOM AND TRIED TO ENTANGLE HIM IN THE PLOT AGAINST FDR.
HERE'S A LITTLE CASH TO COVER YOUR EXPENSES.
EIGHTEEN THOUSAND DOLLAR BILLS
TAKE IT BACK - I DON'T WANT YOUR DAMN MONEY!
SPAIN '05

Act 7

THE PLOT AGAINST
AMERICA

NEWTOWN SQUARE, PENNSYLVANIA, JULY 1933

When he was not marching across America, Butler enjoyed lounging at home with Ethel, their grown children and a growing brood of grandchildren. He loved women, children and pets and was generally surrounded by armies of them. He was particularly close to his grown daughter, Snooks, who—like her parents—was a tough bird who had kept the family military tradition going by marrying a young marine aviator. At home, Butler often could be found sprawled in his favorite living room armchair, smoking one of his inevitable cigarettes, with a ball of feline fur purring luxuriously in his lap.

The Butlers lived among the country estates of Philadelphia's horse-riding gentry. But from the outside, their own house—a converted wood-and-stucco farmhouse—was a picture of Quaker simplicity. The lush garden was Ethel's one extravagance—everything she planted was red, white or blue.

The living room was the general's showcase, stuffed with the exotic mementos of a dozen overseas campaigns. The room was more like the jumble of an archeology professor's study or a bohemian's opium den than the trophy room of an imperial officer. Two giant ceremonial umbrellas—bestowed on him by grateful Chinese villagers for his restrained and civil rule during his 1927 mission—towered over the room on tall poles; the walls were draped with banners, scrolls, plaques and other decorative flotsam from his global expeditions; an Oriental rug covered the entire floor; Chinese silk screens adorned with growling

Butler FAWNED OVER HIS PETS AND GRANDCHILDREN, BUT DUTY STILL CALLED.

tigers stood sentry in the corners; a fireplace and two big candelabras bathed the room in a soft, old-world light.

It was in this sanctuary where Smedley Butler greeted two mysterious visitors one summer evening. They were both veterans of the Great War—one said he still had a silver plate in his head. As was his custom with the many ex-soldiers who called upon Butler at his home, the general welcomed them politely. But he soon realized that these men—who had glided up his gravel driveway in a Packard limousine—were not the usual hard-luck vets who visited him.

One introduced himself as Bill Doyle, an official of the American Legion—a veterans' group with whom Butler had often crossed swords. Founded by conservative millionaires, the legion was used by employers to break strikes and advance a reactionary agenda. The other visitor—who did most of the talking—was a corpulent, 35-year-old Wall Street bond salesman named Gerald MacGuire.

Like a good salesman, MacGuire—a perspiring, jowly man with limpid blue eyes—took his sweet time getting to his pitch. MacGuire and his companion chatted amiably for two hours with Butler, but the general still had trouble grasping exactly what they were getting at. As far as Butler could make out, the two men seemed to want to enlist him in a takeover of the American Legion. "We represent the plain soldiers," they told him, and they were unhappy with how the legion's wealthy founders—known as "the royal family"—were dominating the group.

"Right away," Butler later recalled, "I smelled a rat." No average-Joe veterans he knew dressed in bankers' suits and rode around in limousines. The general was a man of the world. As a soldier and a cop, he had danced around with all types of humanity. He began to suspect that his two visitors were front men for a scheme much bigger than they were. Butler decided to play along to find out more.

Over the following year, Gerald MacGuire continued to drop in and out of Butler's life, meeting him at his home, at hotels, even on a train platform. As they talked, the true story behind MacGuire's odd courtship of Butler slowly emerged. It turned out that, as Butler suspected, the fat stockbroker was not simply a pal of the common veteran. MacGuire worked for a prominent Wall Street banker named Colonel Grayson Mallet-Prevost

Murphy, a man who—as a director of the Morgan-owned bank Guaranty Trust and industrial giants like Bethlehem Steel and Goodyear Tire and Rubber—sat at the very apex of American capitalism. Murphy also turned out to be a cofounder of the American Legion, which he had modeled on the proto-fascist European veterans' groups that were used to suppress popular revolts after the war. He was, in other words, one of the "royals" whom MacGuire had pretended to attack in his first meeting with Butler.

As MacGuire came to trust Butler, he revealed more about his mission. He told him that Colonel Murphy, his wealthy employer, was working with a group of other powerful men in the financial and corporate worlds to build "a super organization to maintain democracy." These men, the bond salesman said, were increasingly concerned about President Roosevelt's policies, which they considered "socialistic." They were deeply alarmed by how Roosevelt was abandoning the gold standard and increasing the supply of paper money to create government jobs for the poor. They feared FDR's inflationary policies would shrink their fortunes and bankrupt the nation. They called him "a traitor to his class"—they said he was taking the country down the same road as Russia. Something drastic had to be done to save America.

Butler was stunned and infuriated by what he was hearing. But he tried to keep his famous

FDR's POPULISM ANGERED THE RICH, WHO CALLED HIM "A TRAITOR TO HIS CLASS."

temper in check—he needed to know more. What did these people want with him? Butler asked MacGuire.

They wanted Butler to lead the super organization. They wanted him to mobilize 500,000 veterans and march on Washington. They knew he could do it—they had seen him at work during the Bonus March and at veterans' rallies across America. The show of force would compel President Roosevelt to step aside, and Butler would be installed as a "secretary of general affairs" to run the country along with a committee of Wall Street financiers.

"You know," MacGuire told him, "the American people will swallow that. We have got the newspapers. We will start a campaign that the president's health is failing. Everybody can tell that by looking at him, and the dumb American people will fall for it in a second."

MacGuire told Butler that he had recently attended a meeting of the plotters held in the Paris offices of J.P. Morgan and Company, the most powerful bank on Wall Sreet. The Morgan bank was a hotbed of anti–New Deal passion. The old lion himself—J. P. "Jack" Morgan—thought FDR was a radical "crazy man" with a vendetta against the House of Morgan. After Roosevelt's election, Morgan

bankers suddenly lost their high-level access at the White House and found themselves the targets of aggressive Senate investigations. Jack Morgan's hatred for Roosevelt was so extreme that the banker's servants snipped photos of FDR out of his morning newspapers to keep his blood pressure down.

At the Paris meeting, the Morgan bankers expressed skepticism about Butler as the coup leader. "The Morgan interests say that you cannot be trusted, that you will be too radical, that you are too much on the side of the little fellow," MacGuire told Butler. The Morgan men wanted Doug MacArthur to lead the revolt—now *there* was a man cut out to be a Caesar. But MacGuire—and his boss, Colonel Murphy—had fought in the World War. They knew the mood of the veterans. They told the Morgan group that Smedley Butler was "the only fellow in America who can get the soldiers together."

Butler pushed MacGuire to see if his people were truly serious about financing a coup.

"Don't you know this will cost money?"

"Yes," MacGuire replied, "we have got $3 million to start with, on the line, and we can get $300 million if we need it."

Butler leaned harder on MacGuire to find out whether there really was any cash behind all his talk. "You're bluffing," he gruffly told MacGuire one day when the stockbroker dropped by his hotel room in

MACGUIRE WANTED BUTLER TO LEAD AN ARMED TAKEOVER OF WASHINGTON.

Newark, where the general was speaking to a Veterans of Foreign Wars meeting.

In response, MacGuire simply reached into his wallet and scattered a handful of thousand-dollar bills on his bed—18 in all—and told Butler he could use the money for expenses. The general, who had stayed clean throughout his days in bootleg Philadelphia, exploded. He thought he was being set up. He barked at MacGuire to take back his money. Then, getting control of his anger, he told the broker he simply was tired of dealing with go-betweens. He wanted to start talking to the big operators behind the plot.

To Butler's surprise, MacGuire produced a big fish—sending a millionaire named Robert S. Clark, an heir to the Singer sewing fortune, to meet with the general in his home. Clark told Butler, with whom he had served during the Boxer campaign, that he was willing to spend as much as half of his personal fortune, which totaled $30 million, to put the country on a different course.

Butler sought further assurance about MacGuire's authenticity—and his sanity—by bringing in Paul Comly French, a newspaper reporter whom he knew and respected from his old Philadelphia crime-fighting days. French, a star reporter for the *Philadelphia Record* and the *New York Post*, set up a meeting with MacGuire in his office, at the Wall Street firm of Grayson M-P Murphy & Company. At first, French later noted, the broker was "somewhat cagey," but he grew more expansive as time went by. By the end of their lengthy conversation, MacGuire had confided the outlines of the plot to French, telling him that "we need a fascist government in this country to save the nation from the communists who want to tear it down.

"The only men who have the patriotism to do it are the soldiers," MacGuire added, "and Smedley Butler is the ideal leader. He could organize a million men overnight."

Butler was becoming convinced that Gerald MacGuire was not a con artist, that the plot was real and it was dangerous.

The final confirmation came one morning in September 1934, when Butler opened up his newspaper. A couple of weeks before, MacGuire had told Butler that the "super organization" to overthrow the Roosevelt presidency would be announced soon. The Wall Street man predicted that it would be described benignly, as a society "to maintain the Constitution." Now, staring at the newspaper in his well-worn armchair, a chill ran up the general's spine.

There it was—a story about the American Liberty League, a new association of prominent bankers and industrialists, dedicated to "combating radicalism, preserving property rights and upholding the Constitution." The treasurer of the new organization was none other than Colonel Grayson M-P Murphy; one of its financiers was Robert S. Clark; and one of its executive committee members was John W. Davis, chief attorney for J. P. Morgan, onetime Democratic presidential

THE LEAGUE WAS A CAULDRON OF ANTI-ROOSEVELT AGITATION.

nominee and a man often mentioned by MacGuire.

The Liberty League immediately aimed fire at FDR, charging that he had "betrayed the oath of his office" and comparing his New Deal to "the Five-Year Plans of the Soviet Government." Despite the league's fiery rhetoric, the organization's chairman—a former Democratic Party official—hollowly assured the press that he sympathized with Roosevelt. In fact, he told the press, if the president ever needed to crack down on radical extremists, he could count on the league to mobilize as many as three million patriots to defend Washington. To Butler, that sounded more like a direct threat than a show of support. This was clearly the army of disgruntled veterans that he was supposed to lead into the capital—to persuade the president that, in the interest of the country, he should accept a ceremonial role, while a council of military men and bankers took command of the ship of state.

Wall Street greeted the Liberty League "like an answer to a prayer," according to the *New York Times.* Among the league's supporters were some of the biggest names in American finance and industry, beginning with Morgan-affiliated bankers and lawyers like Murphy and Davis. Butler was alarmed to read that the powerful DuPont family, one of the greatest beneficiaries of the World War, were the Liberty League's main financial backers. With the DuPonts' generous support, the organization quickly established itself as the most lavishly funded political lobby in the country.

Something ominous was happening in America, Butler reflected. First the war, then the Prohibition crime wave, and now the Depression—these cataclysms had thrown the country off center, unleashing the kind of passions that could devour something as fragile as a democracy. The desperate classes were driven to the left, where many found relief in the intoxicating elixirs of Marxism, radio demagoguery and utopian preachings. Meanwhile, the ruling classes, terrified of the growing social upheaval, began flirting openly with fascist solutions.

Madness was in the air. Fascist groups modeled on European stormtroopers suddenly bullied their way into the spotlight, arming themselves and declaring war on FDR's "Jew Deal." Some—like the Silver Shirts, run by the oddball William Dudley Pelley—were hard to take seriously. Pelley was an American gothic original, a spiritualist and screenwriter whose failed career in "Jewish" Hollywood fueled his anti-Semitic passions. Pelley spewed hate and flirted with Hitler's government, but he was more interested in fleecing his followers than in building a fascist movement.

Groups like the Black Legion were more ominous. A well-organized terrorist group with roots in the Ku Klux Klan, its members wore black hoods and robes emblazoned with skulls and crossbones, and targeted

THEY MURDERED AT MIDNIGHT!

HUMPHREY **BOGART**

BLACK LEGION

ANN SHERIDAN

UNMASKING AMERICA'S BROTHERHOOD OF BUTCHERY!

THE WAVE OF FASCIST TERROR INSPIRED A BOGART MOVIE.

Jews, Catholics, blacks, union organizers and Democratic officeholders. The legion cut a violent swath through the Midwest in the mid-1930s, particularly in the Detroit area, where its "torch squads" murdered dozens of black people, set fire to the homes of political opponents, plotted assassinations of pro–New Deal city officials and conspired to contaminate with typhoid germs the milk and cheese delivered to Jewish families.

The black-hooded gang drew screaming headlines and even inspired a 1937 Humphrey Bogart movie, *Black Legion*. It stirred deep anxieties, not only because of its vicious tactics but because its ranks contained many state and local officials, as well as law enforcement officers. The legion also seemed particularly sinister because it was funded by major industrialists, including—once again—the DuPonts. The Delaware dynasty, which in addition to its chemical company also controlled General Motors, used the hooded thugs to terrorize auto-union organizers, beating some of them to death and firebombing their union halls.

The DuPont family seemed especially receptive to the feverish ideas that were sweeping through wealthy circles during the Roosevelt era. The dynasty, founded by a royal courtier who had fled the French Revolution's guillotine, was built on gunpowder. During the Great War, the company—which by then was run by three brothers, Irénée,

Pierre and Lamott—had reaped such piratical sums that the fraternal trio was called to testify before the Nye committee, a Senate panel investigating war profiteering. (DuPont's yearly profits had soared from $6 million to nearly $60 million during the war.) After the war, though they had helped demolish Germany, the DuPonts were only too happy to collaborate with the Nazi regime in rebuilding the nation's military prowess, pouring millions into the I.G. Farben chemical conglomerate as well as the Krupps arms colossus.

Company president Irénée DuPont was the most formidable member of the clan and the most unbalanced in his thinking. A keen observer of Hitler's rise, he subscribed to the Nazi leader's eugenics theories—despite

his own Jewish heritage—and advocated a bizarre scientific program to build a race of supermen. In testimony before the Nye committee, DuPont declared that in times of crisis, such as war, America needed "an absolute monarch." Democracy was too weak a system when everything was at risk, the chemical mogul told the committee.

These were the sort of men Smedley Butler found himself confronting. Their views were fanatical and their resources were boundless. The old soldier had always detested men like Irénée DuPont whose treasure was made of blood. They would go to any extremes to protect it.

Through most of his career, Butler had done these men's bidding. Now he was about to turn his sword on them.

WHEN TREASON WAS THE RAGE

After Smedley Butler exposed the Wall Street plot, the air was knocked out of the Roosevelt haters. But treasonous rumblings could still be heard from time to time through the remainder of the Roosevelt presidency. After FDR's landslide re-election in 1936, some diehard fanatics held a series of meetings at New York's Warwick Hotel and Cornell Club, where they frothed about the upcoming fascist putsch and how it should be organized.

In 1938, after Major General George Van Horn Moseley—MacArthur's rabid side-kick—retired from the army with a parting blast at the New Deal, goosestepping million-aires thought they had found their Führer. That December, Moseley—a raging anti-Semite who thought Jews should be stripped of their civil liberties—lit up a prosperous crowd of Roosevelt-haters in the Empire Room of the Waldorf-Astoria with an incendiary speech. Moseley threatened to mobilize an army of "patriots" to eliminate "our domestic enemies." The resulting blood-bath, he vowed, would "make those massacres now recorded in history look like peaceful church parades."

Moseley warned that New York and Washington might have to be burned in the process. "It might be one way of reducing the bureaucracy," sneered the general, as the well-heeled businessmen cheered.

And in 1940, following FDR's unprecedented third-term election, high society again worked itself into a traitorous fever. Cornelius Vanderbilt, Jr.—the socialite and newspaperman who leaked the story about Mussolini's road carnage—was well-positioned to hear such treasonous chatter, since he was a habitué of Newport and Fifth Avenue soirees. Van-derbilt was alarmed to hear seri-ous talk in these circles of a plot to kidnap Roosevelt and install an authoritarian regime. The conspirators included tycoons as well as army officers.

Vanderbilt, who was an ardent New Deal sup-porter, tipped off Eleanor Roosevelt. The plot, he later wrote in his mem-oir, was then disposed of in a clubby sort of way that was typical of FDR. "When the facts were known, I was per-mitted to call my friends [in the army] and offer a tip that all the plans were known. Those in-volved in the cabal were not disgraced or down-graded, but they weren't promoted either."

FDR loyalist Cornelius Vanderbilt, Jr., top, and the treasonous Major General George Van Horn Moseley

New York City, November 1934

Smedley Butler, looking grimly determined, strode through the colonnaded entry of the New York Bar Association Building on West 44th Street. Making his way to a banquet room, he sat down at a table facing a panel of men all wearing their own sober expressions and was promptly sworn in. The House Un-American Activities Committee was in special session, presided over by Rep. John W. McCormack of Massachusetts, future speaker of the house, and his vice-chairman, Rep. Samuel Dickstein, a future New York Supreme Court justice.

After months of playing along with the anti-Roosevelt plotters, Butler was finally exposing their clandestine machinations. By joining the conspiracy, he could have made himself rich and powerful. But he was choosing the path of honor.

He knew that he was taking on some of the most formidable men in the country. He knew that they, and their friends in the press, would react with titanic fury. But the old soldier was never one to shirk his duty.

Before starting his testimony, Butler addressed Chairman McCormack. "May I preface my remarks, sir, by saying that I have one interest in all of this, and that is to try to do my best to see that a democracy is maintained in this country."

"Nobody who has either read about or known about General Butler would have anything but that understanding," McCormack responded.

And then Butler launched into his extraordinary story, a chronicle that revealed how scorned President Roosevelt was in some elite circles and the lengths that some were prepared to go to remove him from office. The committee found it a profoundly disturbing tale, for no representatives of democracy want to hear the wolves' low growl outside the tent. Butler, however, told the story in its full horror. And he did not hesitate to name the powerful conspirators.

The general's testimony was backed up by the reporter Paul Comly French, who added his own unsettling details. French testified that Gerald MacGuire assured him the coup forces would be well-equipped when they stormed Washington—courtesy of Remington Arms, yet another DuPont asset.

When MacGuire was hauled before the committee, he denied everything. He was simply working for a "sound dollar" business campaign, the Wall Street broker told the panel, and he had tried to enlist General Butler as a spokesman. Interviewed by reporters afterwards, MacGuire said, "General Butler must be seeking publicity," and called Butler's testimony "a pacifist stunt."

The other Wall Street figures named by Butler also rejected the accusations with fuming indignation. "A fantasy!" roared Colonel Murphy. "Perfect moonshine!" declared a J. P. Morgan spokesman.

But the committee pressed forward, calling MacGuire back for a second and then a third round of testimony. Each time the broker underwent grilling, his story became more riddled with inconsistencies, memory lapses and outright falsehoods. He could not explain why so much money flowed through his personal bank account, including large sums from Robert S. Clark and other millionaires whom Butler had tied to the plot. When MacGuire insisted he could

IRÉNÉE (LEFT) AND PIERRE DuPONT: THE BROTHERS' HATRED OF THE NEW DEAL DROVE THEM TO EXTREME MEASURES.

not have scattered thousands of dollars on Butler's hotel bed in Newark because he was in Chicago that day, the committee quickly poked holes in his alibi.

The congressional investigators were finding Butler's charges increasingly credible. But, watching from the sidelines, the general was growing frustrated. He wanted the committee to call the "big shots" and put them under oath—men like Colonel Murphy, the DuPonts, John Davis of J. P. Morgan. But the committee leaders were wary of confronting such major figures face to face. They said they needed more evidence.

Meanwhile, with no big-name witnesses, the hearings began to lose steam. Time was running out. Rumors spread in Washington that the committee would never subpoena the bigwigs, that they had cut deals with the Roosevelt Justice Department. In return for not being prosecuted, they had promised to abandon their plot.

As the investigation stalled, Butler was left exposed in enemy territory. He had led the charge, now the return fire was aimed directly at him, and it was withering.

Time magazine, the voice of Henry Luce—flirter with fascism, hater of Roosevelt, coddler of the plutocracy—took the lead in savaging Butler. Instead of investigating his charges, the magazine simply ridiculed the general, as well as Congressmen McCormack and Dickstein for taking him seriously. It was a "plot without plotters," *Time* declared in December, as the committee was wrapping up its investigation—and Butler was a shameless troublemaker. "No military officer of the U.S. since the late, tempestuous George Custer has succeeded in publicly floundering in so much hot water as Smedley Darlington Butler."

The *Washington Post* also mocked Butler's charges, publishing its own "exposé" of an anti-Roosevelt plot that "called for the conspirators to reach Washington by balloons" and then parachute onto the White House lawn.

Undeterred by the derisive press coverage, the committee released its final report the following February—and it completely vindicated Butler. "There is no question," the report concluded, "that certain persons had made an attempt to establish a fascist organization in this country... and [this plan] might have been placed in execution when and if the financial backers deemed it expedient." In addition, the committee stated, it "was able to verify all the pertinent statements made by General Butler."

The language of the report was cautious and restrained, but its conclusions were still explosive: fascist plotters connected to Wall Street had contemplated the overthrow of America's duly elected government. And yet—with the exception of Jewish publications, which greeted the committee's findings with grave seriousness, and a couple of crusading reporters for the left-wing press named John Spivak and George Seldes—the media response was strangely nonchalant.

The *New York Times'* article on the committee report focused on the less shocking aspects of the inquiry. The Butler investigation was buried deep inside the story. A decorated U.S. general had been approached by Wall Street plotters to lead a fascist march on Washington—but the *Times* greeted this rather stunning piece of news as if it were barely fit to print.

Old Devil Dog was red with rage. He had stood up for American democracy, only to be treated with scorn and yawning indifference. He blamed the press, the committee, the Roosevelt administration, and of course, the well-connected conspirators themselves. No one in Washington wanted to confront them and bring them to justice.

The general would not surrender. He would go directly to the American people and warn them of the danger.

Speech Delivered by
GENERAL SMEDLEY D. BUTLER
COLUMBIA BROADCASTING SYSTEM
11 P.M. Sunday, February 17, 1935

———

UN-AMERICAN ACTIVITIES

I am extremely gratified over this opportunity to present to the people of this country some facts which they may otherwise not have known.

Tonight the Columbia network has given me the opportunity to talk to the whole nation on this matter. I can't begin to cover this tremendous subject in the 13 minutes allowed me. I'll only be able to give you a sketchy idea of this movement and I hope that, some time in the near future, I will again have the opportunity to address this nation-wide audience.

One of the things I want to talk to you about right now is that some of the most important portions of my testimony before this Committee have been suppressed in the official report to Congress. Your own Congressmen don't know the whole truth, so I am sure you don't. And these Congressmen are called upon to pass legislation to deal with this situation which the Committee, in its report which I hold in my hand, admits is serious. Why didn't your Committee--you pay for its investigations in your taxes--and the committee has already spent $30,000 of your money and is asking for more--why did your Committee suppress this testimony? Why all this hush-hush business? Why not follow up all the leads? If the Committee believes--and its formal report to Congress says it does believe and has substantiated the testimony that I gave--not only testimony they have published, but all of my testimony, that a plot was afoot to mobilize 500,000 war veterans--why does it, this is the Committee, suppress this testimony and refuse to call important witnesses?

AN AMERICAN NIGHTMARE

Though the nation's press tried to play down the Wall Street plot against FDR, fears of a fascist coup rippled through America's dream life in the wake of Butler's revelations. Several months after Butler's shocking congressional testimony, Nobel Prize–winning novelist Sinclair Lewis began work on *It Can't Happen Here,* in which he imagined a fascist takeover of the United States. The novel—which Lewis wrote in a "white heat…six weeks of furious typing," according to the *New York Times*—became an instant bestseller when it was published in October 1935. MGM bought the movie rights, but then suddenly dropped the project. (Lewis charged the studio caved to pressure from movie industry czar Will Hays, who feared a boycott of Hollywood films in Hitler's Germany and Mussolini's Italy if *It Can't Happen Here* was produced.) Instead, Lewis turned the book into a play, which was produced by FDR's Federal Theatre Project in 18 cities, including a Yiddish version in New York and a Seattle production with an all-black cast. "If we ever have fascism in this country," Lewis told the press, "it will come as a result of the activities of the economic royalists… such organizations as the Liberty League."

Hollywood did grapple with the nightmarish scenario of a fascist coup in *The President Vanishes,* which—in a strange twist—was released in December 1934, shortly after Butler exposed the plot against Roosevelt. The producers of the film took

pains to run a disclaimer in the opening credits—"This dramatic episode is in no sense historical." But coming after the Wall Street plot headlines, the movie still proved disturbing. The story involved a peace-loving president who engineers his own disappearance in a desperate bid to foil a conspiracy by a cabal of tycoons, who are intent on driving the country to war. The president's wealthy foes connive to take power with the help of an army of street thugs called the Grey Shirts. The parallels with contemporary events were obvious. When a Secret Service agent loyal to the president surprises the corporate conspirators and shoots one of them in the leg, one of the cabal wisecracks, "Well, boys, how do you like the New Deal now?"

In March 1941, with Europe under Hitler's boot, director Frank Capra released *Meet John Doe,* in which an everyman hero played by Gary Cooper confronts a big-bellied corporate villain (Edward Arnold, of course) with a paramilitary army and a lust for dictatorship. The scenes where Arnold shows off his jackbooted motorcyle corps have the menacing darkness of a newsreel. Capra later wrote that he made the movie because "little 'Führers' were springing up in America, to proclaim that freedom was weak, sterile, passé."

✦✦✦ Devil Dog ✦✦✦

General Smedley Butler was sitting at his desk in his cluttered study, hunched over a radio microphone, speaking to a nationwide audience over the CBS network. It was 11 o'clock on a Sunday night, and most of the country was preparing for bed. But the general, who was in full growl, was doing his damnedest to wake everyone up.

Butler was addressing the country about the recent House Un-American Activities Committee investigation, and he jumped right in by posing a series of uncomfortable questions about the probe.

Why was this investigation conducted behind closed doors?

Why were some of the most important portions of my testimony suppressed in the official report?

Why didn't this committee call all the important figures mentioned in my testimony—men like Colonel Grayson M. P. Murphy and General Douglas MacArthur?

The plot against democracy involved some of the biggest names on Wall Street, Butler made clear. "This was no piker set-up. This was no shoestring khaki shirt fascist movement."

Men like this thought they were beyond scrutiny and above the law. But the American people should not let them get away with it, Butler thundered. "If you are interested in your government, if you are interested in preserving your democracy, if you are opposed to all un-American activities, don't let this thing drop. Don't let the big shots of this un-American plot go forever unquestioned."

The month before, Butler had signed a deal with his local radio station to broadcast 15-minute commentaries from his home on a topic broadly defined as "real American patriotism." The free-swinging Butler broadcasts, which were fed into the national CBS network, soon developed an ardent audience. During the first weeks of the show, Butler steered clear of the Wall Street plot investigation, honoring Rep. McCormack's request to keep mum in public. But after the committee's weak-kneed performance, Butler decided to lay bare the whole sordid affair to the American people, using his radio show as his platform.

Butler's broadside ignited an explosive response from his radio audience.

"I believe your name will go down in History as another Paul Revere," a listener in Delaware wrote the general. "*Don't Stop.* They will suppress you if possible, but they don't know the *Fighting Marine*, do they?"

"As a former enlisted man in that greatest of all American military service branches—the United States Marine Corps—I wish to state that I am inordinately proud of the fact that my old commander stood by Old Glory," wrote a Chicago listener. "You were literally true to the cherished Marine Corps motto, *Semper Fidelis*, and refused to enter into any treasonable conspiracies with the enemies of our country, the filthy money changers of Wall Street."

Veterans across the country rallied around Butler. Declarations of support were issued by numerous Veterans of Foreign Wars posts, and VFW president James Van Zandt gave further credence to Butler's charges by revealing that he too had been approached by the Wall Street plotters.

Meanwhile, President Roosevelt maneuvered artfully against his enemies in his own quietly effective way. The Wall Street plotters were visited by FBI agents and notified that they were under surveillance for treasonous activities. And FDR's nemesis, General MacArthur—who had clashed repeatedly with the president over military budget cuts and New Deal spending—was abruptly informed that he was not being reappointed as army chief of staff. Instead, the imperious general—who had assured the plotters that the army would not interfere if they seized the reins of power in Washington—was reduced in rank and shipped overseas to the Philippines. MacArthur would spend the rest of Roosevelt's presidency commanding troops in Asia, exiled from the capital like a disloyal Roman general.

As the 1936 presidential campaign season began, Roosevelt's enemies shifted to the electoral battlefield, using the Liberty League as their primary weapon. Even though congressional investigators had shied away from a showdown with the DuPonts and the league's other founders, Butler had done his best to connect them to the plot. As league officials launched their well-financed offensive against FDR, an unpleasant whiff of treason clung to their efforts. The league seemed more like a den of un-American intrigue than a noble champion of free-enterprise values.

President Roosevelt's campaign team capitalized on the Liberty League's public image problem, with James Farley, Democratic National Committee chairman, flaying the millionaire club as the country's very "center of predatory powers."

The Liberty League "would rule America," Farley told a Democratic banquet in Miami in February 1936—and anyone who had followed the Butler affair knew exactly what he meant. "It would squeeze the worker dry in his old age and cast him like an orange rind into the refuse pail."

These Liberty League "Bourbons" were so blindly greedy, Farley continued, they did not even realize that the man in the White House whom they so reviled had saved their skins. The Roosevelt administration's "whole successful effort has been to save and restore business and it has accomplished that very thing, just as it has removed the great mass of our people from the jeopardy of economic destruction."

FDR's usual choice of weapons in attacking his wealthy opponents was a scalpel-like wit. During the last whirl of the campaign, he passed through Wilmington, capital of the chemical dynasty—"just to assure myself that the DuPonts are not broke," he cracked. Roosevelt liked to tell the story of the rich man who fell in the river. A brave passerby jumped in and rescued him. But once he was dripping safely on shore, the wealthy fellow berated the man for not saving his silk top hat too.

In his final campaign speech, delivered to a roaring crowd packed into Madison Square Garden, Roosevelt dropped the scalpel and picked up a populist club—using it to beat his top-hatted enemies into the ground. Throughout the Roaring '20s, FDR declared, these plutocrats had worshipped "the golden calf" and the country was forced to pay for their money lust. "Nine crazy years at the ticker and three long years in the breadlines!" Now these selfish souls were trying to restore their regime, "with its doctrine that the government is best which is most indifferent." But, Roosevelt shouted to the ecstatic arena, he was not going to let them.

"Never before in all history have these forces been so united against one candidate as they stand today. They are unanimous in their hatred for me—*and I welcome their hatred.*"

> **Roosevelt EXILED the mutinous MacArthur to the FAR EAST.**

If the Liberty League did not understand why Franklin Roosevelt was essential for the country's survival, American voters did. On November 3, FDR won a crushing victory over his Republican opponent, Alf Landon, even taking the Kansas governor's own state. The humiliating defeat also broke the back of the league, which had poured a fortune into the campaign against Roosevelt. All that money, all that spleen—and in the end, it amounted to nothing. By 1938, even the daughter of Jouett Shouse, the Liberty League's high-paid chief, had gone to work for Roosevelt's New Deal. Soon afterwards, the league faded into oblivion, and along with it, the Wall Street conspirators' hopes for overthrowing the Roosevelt revolution.

BASHING THE CULT OF **GREED, FDR** SWEPT TO REELECTION.

As the decade drew to a close, Roosevelt headed toward an unprecedented third-term victory. American democracy seemed much more secure than it had been just a few tumultuous years before. For that, the American people owed a debt of gratitude to a man who had fought bravely for his country in war and peace.

Many years after the Wall Street affair, John W. McCormack was visited by a newspaperwoman in his Boston office, where, at age 81, he still conducted business. McCormack was retired from politics, but the man who had reached the pinnacle of Congress—as speaker of the house during the Kennedy, Johnson and Nixon administrations—was keen and quick-witted as he reminisced about his long career. McCormack had witnessed many crises and calamities during his years in Washington, from wars to assassinations to presidential scandals. But that day, he wanted to talk about a threat to American democracy that few had heard about. And, leaning back in his chair, the tall, silver-haired Boston Irishman lit up a thin cigar and told his story.

It was the story of a long-forgotten general who had saved America.

"I cannot emphasize too strongly the very important part the general, hero of the marines, played in stopping this attempt to overthrow the government. If he had not been such a stubborn devotee of democracy, Americans today could conceivably be living under an American Mussolini, Hitler or Franco."

The general had not always been kind to McCormack and his committee. He had tongue-lashed them for not conducting a more aggressive investigation. But none of that mattered to McCormack now. He was speaking for the historical record. And he wanted his fellow citizens to know.

The general's name was Smedley Darlington Butler. And he was an American hero.

Boys dream of war. But Smedley Butler

outgrew these dreams.

"As a youngster, I loved the excitement of battle," he told a reporter in the last years of his life. "It's lots of fun, you know, and it's nice to strut around in front of your wife—or somebody else's wife—and display your medals and your uniform. But there's another side to it," he added, in a way that made it clear he'd seen far too much of that side. And that's why he had devoted the rest of his life to stopping war—and to exposing those who grew as fat as ticks off its endless blood.

When tensions arose in 1937 over the sinking of a U.S. gunboat while it was accompanying three Standard Oil tankers on China's Yangtze River, Butler declared that American forces had no business there. "Why don't those damned oil companies fly their own flags on their personal property—maybe a flag with a gas pump on it!" he exploded.

But as Hitler's juggernaut menaced Europe, Butler clearly wrestled with his antiwar convictions, including his vow never again to fight on foreign soil. The vehemence of these convictions was matched by the fervor of his antifascism. In the end, the Butler family once again did its duty, and both of Smedley's sons, as well as his son-in-law, all served with honor in World War II.

Butler himself would probably have approved their enlistment, although with a suffering heart. But by then he was gone. The old soldier died on June 21, 1940, after checking into Philadelphia Navy Yard hospital, complaining of exhaustion from the rigors of another speaking tour. Doctors diagnosed what seemed to be stomach cancer. He was 58 years old.

After a lifetime of service to his country, he left behind an estate totaling $2,000, which shows why a man's value can never be measured by his wealth.

Press obituaries gloried in Butler's heroism and the picaresque details of his military career. But they ignored his evolution into an antiwar crusader, and they barely mentioned the Wall Street plot. During the war, the Hearst newspaper chain—no fan of Butler in life—turned him into a cartoon action hero, as a swashbuckling character in its comic series "Heroes of Democracy." Butler was shown in one cartoon panel belligerently shouting, "1,000 Marines can whip 10,000 of any other soldiers!"

Butler would have been dismayed by his strange ghost life in America. After the war, his worst fears seemed to come true, as the "war racket" grew into the military-industrial complex and the world threatened itself with extinction. The man who saved America would surely have wished a different fate for his country.

So here's how we will end our story of General Smedley Butler.

Boys dream of war. But men can dream of peace.

FURTHER READING

SMEDLEY DARLINGTON BUTLER

War Is a Racket. By Brigadier General Smedley D. Butler. Los Angeles: Feral House, 2003

Old Gimlet Eye: The Adventures of Smedley D. Butler. By Lowell Thomas. New York: Farrar & Rinehart, 1933

Maverick Marine: General Smedley D. Butler and the Contradictions of American Military History. By Hans Schmidt. Lexington: The University Press of Kentucky, 1998

CHINA

The Boxer Rebellion: The Dramatic Story of China's War on Foreigners That Shook the World in the Summer of 1900. By Diana Preston. New York: Berkley Books, 2000

Dragon Lady: The Life and Legend of the Last Empress of China. By Sterling Seagrave. New York: Vintage Books, 1993

NICARAGUA

Confronting the American Dream: Nicaragua Under U.S. Imperial Rule. By Michel Gobat. Durham and London: Duke University Press, 2005

HAITI

Taking Haiti: Military Occupation and the Culture of U.S. Imperialism, 1915–1940. By Mary A. Renda. Chapel Hill and London: University of North Carolina Press, 2001

WORLD WAR I

The Illusion of Victory: America in World War I. By Thomas Fleming. New York: Basic Books, 2004

THE BONUS ARMY MARCH

The Bonus Army: An American Epic. By Paul Dickson and Thomas B. Allen. New York: Walker & Company, 2004

THE PLOT AGAINST FDR

The Plot to Seize the White House: The Shocking True Story of the Conspiracy to Overthrow FDR. By Jules Archer. New York: Skyhorse Publishing, 2007

Trading with the Enemy: The Nazi-American Money Plot, 1933–1949. By Charles Higham. An Authors Guild Backinprint .com Edition, 2007

It Can't Happen Here. By Sinclair Lewis. New York: New American Library, 2005

FDR. By Jean Edward Smith. New York: Random House, 2008

American Caesar: Douglas MacArthur, 1880–1964. By William Manchester. New York: Back Bay Books, 2008

The House of Morgan: An American Banking Dynasty and the Rise of Modern Finance. By Ron Chernow. New York: Atlantic Monthly Press, 1990

Lords of Finance: The Bankers Who Broke the World. By Liaquat Ahamed. New York: The Penguin Press, 2009

Picture Credits

Contents page: Illustration by Spain Rodriguez

Page 15: Young Smedley Darlington Butler, courtesy of the Smedley Butler Estate

Page 16: Illustration by Spain Rodriguez

Page 18: Map of Smedley Butler's Long March by Norma Tennis

Page 19: Women in China, *Harper's Weekly,* August 25, 1900

Page 20: Demon with dagger, the *Sunday World,* copyright 1898 by
The Press Publishing Co.

Page 22: Illustration by Spain Rodriguez

Page 24: Boxer allies, photo by Hulton Archive/Getty Images

Page 24: U.S. soldiers in Signal Corps, photo by Time Life Pictures/US Army/National
Archives/Time Life Pictures/Getty Images

Page 25: *Harper's Weekly* cover, July 28, 1900

Page 26: Illustration by Spain Rodriguez

Page 28: Teddy Roosevelt and Mark Twain, *Puck,* September 12, 1900

Page 29: Boxer prisoners, courtesy of the Library of Congress

Page 30: Empress Dowager, painting by unknown artist, circa 1903

Page 32: Illustration by Spain Rodriguez

Page 34: Butler wedding announcement, *Philadelphia Inquirer*

Page 36: Teddy Roosevelt, H.C. White

Page 37: Panama Canal postcard, courtesy of the Clive Fennessy Collection

Page 38: Map of Nicaragua by Norma Tennis

Page 38: Toucan, courtesy of WallsoftheWild.com Giant Wildlife Mural Stickers

Page 39: Illustration by Spain Rodriguez

Page 40: Seated Marines, courtesy of the U.S. Marine Corps archives, Quantico,
Virginia

Page 41: Marine in front of train, courtesy of the U.S. Marine Corps archives,
Quantico, Virginia

Page 42: Illustration by Spain Rodriguez

Page 43: Illustration by Spain Rodriguez

Page 44: Marine poster, courtesy of the U.S. Marine Corps archives, Quantico,
Virginia

Page 45: Bulldog poster, courtesy of the U.S. Marine Corps archives, Quantico, Virginia

Page 46: Portrait of Ruben Darío, Archivo General de la Nación, Buenos Aires

Page 48: Illustration by Spain Rodriguez

Page 52: Illustration by Spain Rodriguez

Page 54: Illustration by Spain Rodriguez

Page 55: Caco Rebel, courtesy of the U.S. Marine Corps archives, Quantico, Virginia

Page 56: Postcard of Port-au-Prince, Haiti, Raphael Tuck & Sons, 1905

Page 56: Photo of marine camp in Haiti, courtesy of the U.S. Marine Corps archives, Quantico, Virginia

Page 58: Map of Haiti by Norma Tennis

Page 60: Nude Haitian woman, courtesy of the U.S. Marine Corps archives, Quantico, Virginia

Page 61: Photo of combat in Haiti, courtesy of the U.S. Marine Corps archives, Quantico, Virginia

Page 62: Illustration by Spain Rodriguez

Page 66: Illustration by Spain Rodriguez

Page 70: Enlistment poster, courtesy of Gary Borkan, www.rare-posters.com

Page 72: "Let's Go" poster, courtesy of the U.S. Marine Corps archive, Quantico, Virginia

Page 72: Butler crossing Atlantic, courtesy of the U.S. Marine Corps archives, Quantico, Virginia

Page 73: Camp at Brest, France, courtesy of the U.S. Marine Corps archives, Quantico, Virginia

Page 74–75: Map of northern France by Norma Tennis

Page 76: Illustration by Spain Rodriguez

Page 78: Nieuport 28 fighter plane, illustration © 1988 by Jim Alley

Page 79: Teddy Roosevelt with son Quentin, courtesy of the Library of Congress

Page 80: Teufel Hunden poster, courtesy of Gary Borkan, www.rare-posters.com

Page 82–83: Illustration by Spain Rodriguez

Page 84: Otto Dix, "Shock Troops Advance under Gas" *(Sturmtruppe geht unter Gas vor)* © 2010 Artists Rights Society (ARS), New York/VG Bild-Kunst, Bonn

Page 86: Mary Roberts Rinehart, photo by Topical Press Agency/Getty Images

Page 89: "First to Fight" poster by Spain Rodriguez

Page 90: Dalton Trumbo photo by Cleo Trumbo, courtesy of the Trumbo family

Page 91: Photo of disfigured veteran from World War I, photo © Albert Harlingue/ Roger-Viollet/The Image Works

Page 92: Illustration by Spain Rodriguez

Page 94: Frank McHugh, James Cagney and Humphrey Bogart, still from *The Roaring Twenties*, Warner Brothers

Page 95: Cops raiding a still, courtesy National Archives and Records Administration

Page 97: Bobbed Hair Bandits, *Judge,* 1923

Page 98: Illustration by Spain Rodriguez

Page 101: Bal Masque Flappers, *Judge,* 1923

Page 102: Party illustration, *Vanity Fair,* 1923

Page 104: Basement bootleg raid, photo © Underwood & Underwood/Corbis

Page 106: Philadelphia Mayor William Vare, U.S. Senate Historical Office

Page 110: Illustration by Spain Rodriguez

Page 114: Herbert Hoover, courtesy of the National Archives and Records Administration

Page 116: Bonus Army Camp, courtesy of the Library of Congress

Page 117: Pierre DuPont, General Motors

Page 118: illustration by Spain Rodriguez

Page 120: General Douglas MacArthur in 1918, photo by Ralph Estem

Page 121: Flag from Bonus Army camp

Page 122: Smedley Butler giving a speech, courtesy of the U.S. Marine Corps archives, Quantico, Virginia

Page 123: KKK letter to Butler, courtesy of the U.S. Marine Corps archives, Quantico, Virginia

Page 123: Jewish Basketball League letter to Butler, courtesy of the U.S. Marine Corps archives, Quantico, Virginia

Page 124–25: Union Pacific brochure, courtesy of the U.S. Marine Corps archives, Quantico, Virginia

Page 127: First edition, 1935, of "War Is a Racket" by Smedley D. Butler, Round Table Press, New York

Page 128: Illustration by Spain Rodriguez

Page 130: Butler petting cat, courtesy of the U.S. Marine Corps archives, Quantico, Virginia

Page 130: Butler with family, courtesy of the U.S. Marine Corps archives, Quantico, Virginia

Page 131: FDR with farmers, photo © Bettmann/Corbis

Page 132: Gerry MacGuire, photo © Bettmann/Corbis

Page 135: Illustration by Spain Rodriguez

Page 136: Cornelius Vanderbilt, photo by Hulton Archive/Getty Images

Page 138: The DuPonts, photo by Francis Miller/Time Life Pictures/Getty Images

Page 143: FDR photo by Popperfoto/Getty Images

Page 144: Major General Smedley Darlington Butler, portrait taken late in life, courtesy of the U.S. Marine Corps archives, Quantico, Virginia

About the Author

HAILED AS A "PIONEER OF ONLINE JOURNALISM" by *The New York Times,* David Talbot is the founder and former editor in chief of *Salon.* He is the author of the bestseller *Brothers: The Hidden History of the Kennedy Years.* He has worked as a senior editor for *Mother Jones* magazine, and has written for *The New Yorker, Rolling Stone, Time,* and other publications. Talbot is the cocreator—with his sister, *New Yorker* magazine writer Margaret Talbot—of the Pulp History series.

About the Illustrator

ONE OF THE MOST HIGHLY REGARDED graphic artists to come from the underground comics scene in the United States, Spain Rodriguez is the author and illustrator of *Che: A Graphic Biography* and the creator of the cult-classic Trashman character. He drew the *Dark Hotel* series for *Salon.*

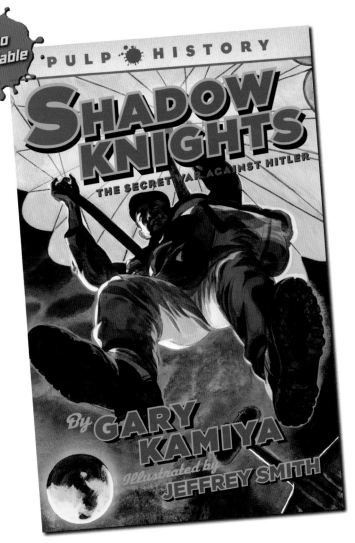

PULP ✹ HISTORY

SHADOW KNIGHTS

THE SECRET WAR AGAINST HITLER

By GARY KAMIYA

Illustrated by JEFFREY SMITH

Shadow Knights

By Gary Kamiya
Illustrated by Jeffrey Smith

*The exhilarating, illustrated story of the everyday men
and women who risked their lives to sabotage Hitler
in occupied Europe.*

In the darkest days of World War II, Churchill created a top-secret organization to subvert Hitler—to "set Europe ablaze." Its agents were chosen from the general public and endured strenuous physical and mental tests. One in four would not return from their missions. *Shadow Knights* depicts the thrilling transformation of schoolteachers and writers to undercover operatives, and the unmistakable impact their personal courage had on World War II.